Managing for Success

MANAGING FOR SUCCESS

PRACTICAL ADVICE FOR MANAGERS

STEVEN R. SMITH

CAMBRIDGE HILL PRESS

First Edition Copyright © 2014 by Steven R. Smith
ISBN: 978-0-9897488-0-3
Cambridge Hill Press
Petaluma, California

For more information see our website: SuccessfulManaging.com

Typesetting services by BOOKOW.COM

Contents

Preface

STATISTICS show that 40 percent of new managers fail. Within 18 months they are demoted or terminated, they resign, or they are otherwise performing below expectations. Even among the 60 percent who survive, most are in effect poor managers. Only a lucky few exceed upper management expectations.

Poor management is the top reason for employee turnover, and turnover is very expensive when you consider the time and cost of screening, hiring, and training replacements, as well as the loss of productivity until the new hires become fully efficient.

I have observed managers for 42 years during my career at 15 companies, both large and small. Most of them were fully qualified as far as their professional skills were concerned, but poor at managing people and departments. The reason was simple: they were not trained to manage.

It is disheartening to see otherwise talented managers drive down productivity and lose valuable employees because of poor management skills. They manage as they have been managed, and by emulating their peers, they become poor managers themselves. There is a better way to manage, which is why I decided to write this guide.

Managing for Success is reference guide for daily use mostly for those who manage technical, professional, and other white-collar workers. The book includes the most useful management ideas I have encountered and applied over the years.

When I realized early in my career that I was not trained to manage, I trained myself. I started reading books, attending workshops, and in turn teaching night classes on the subject. While others were reading fiction, I was reading business books on marketing, management, motivation, and leadership. I now have a library of 150 professional books on the subject, many of which have had an influence on my management style and skills.

I know that much of this management training sunk in because, over the years, employees have repeatedly told me I was one of the best managers they ever had, and turnover in my departments was always low. I must have been doing something right.

In Managing for Success I will share with you how I accomplished that: what to do and what not to do and why these practices were successful. Once you understand the rationale for adopting these techniques you are more likely to successfully apply ideas and strategies that work.

Many management books are heavy on theory, light on real-world experiences, and full of fictitious people and scenarios. They end up being long, hard to read, impossible to search, and of little practical value. Many authors are so infatuated with new theories that they ignore the tried-and-true lessons of the past. Not me. This guide will give you the kind of road-tested advice I wish someone had given me when I was in your position.

Why Managers Need Help

Most managers are hired or promoted into their positions because of their professional abilities, not because of their managerial competence or skills. Very few people understand that effective management skills consist of an entirely separate set of skills from those required to succeed in a professional position only.

Over the years I kept running into managers competent in their profession who somehow believed they had the knowledge and skills to manage people and departments without the benefit of management training. This belief is common, but it makes no sense. Having technical skills does not make you a manager. Worse yet, these managers had learned bad management habits from past supervisors and colleagues. No wonder so many of them fail.

If your supervisor appointed you to the position of company pilot, you would immediately say, "Wait a minute! I don't know how to fly a plane. I need training!" But when the same person made you department manager, how did you react? Be honest. It did not even occur to you to ask for management training. But to be effective in your role you need that specialized training and education, just as you do to become an engineer, a scientist, or a pilot. Even if you are the exception, born knowing instinctively how to manage people, you can learn to become even better at it by exploring the ideas and behaviors described in this guide.

What This Guide Can Do for You

This guide will not overload you with information, but will provide you with plainly stated ideas and techniques you can apply to your most important managerial duties. Some aspects of a manager's job are far more important than others. The topics covered in this guide are the ones that I found to be most important for your success.

If you are serious about becoming a better manager, study this guide and keep it handy. If you are good now, you will become better. If you are more typical of today's manager, chances are you are not as good as you think, even though you are doing your best. Don't be afraid to acknowledge that you do not know what you should be doing as a manager, why you should be doing it, or how to do it most effectively.

Once you understand these ideas and practices, you can apply them to your own work and also share them with your direct reports who manage others. When they, too, put them to work your department should really be humming!

Key Concepts for Success

THE four key concepts summarized in this chapter are crucial stepping-stones to build on in order to achieve management success. Much of the content presented later in this guide will link back to them, showing you how they can and should be applied in a variety of contexts that will result in successful outcomes.

The 80/20 Rule

An important aspect of a manager's job is time allocation, and the "80/20 rule" is central to wise decision-making in this area. What it states, in brief, is that approximately 20 percent of causes explain about 80 percent of results in most areas of our lives. Also known as the Pareto Principle, or the Pareto Distribution, the idea was first introduced in 1895 by the Italian economist Wilfredo Pareto. By examining data from several countries across many different topics, Pareto discovered that virtually everything is subject to the 80/20 Rule: For example:

- 20 percent of surnames account for 80 percent of the population.
- 20 percent of people hold 80 percent of the wealth.
- 20 percent of cities contain 80 percent of the population.
- 20 percent of drivers cause 80 percent of accidents.
- 20 percent of products account for 80 percent of sales.
- 20 percent of customers contribute 80 percent of profits.
- 20 percent of clients create 80 percent of headaches.
- 20 percent of friends bring 80 percent of pleasure.

And the list goes on and on. You get the picture. Pareto called the top 20 percent the "vital few" and the bottom 80 percent the "trivial many." If you pay close attention to it, you will find that it applies to almost every aspect of both your personal and professional life. Making decisions based on the 80/20 rule can make a dramatic difference in your efforts to become an effective manager.

The 80/20 rule is counterintuitive in a way. We generally assume that our various tasks, customers, projects, and employees deserve equal time, attention, and effort on our part. This is a crucial mistake, because the majority of results are in fact the product of a small minority of inputs, in a roughly 80/20 relationship.

This rule is referenced throughout this guide because it is so important to your success. Why spend time and effort on the "trivial many" activities when you could be devoting these valuable resources to the "vital few" that will yield most of your results?

Needless to say, these figures are only estimates. The real percentages could be 70/20 or 90/20. What matters is that the general concept: much of what we do matters very little to our outcomes.

Low Value Activities Waste Time

Most people waste considerable time on work that does not contribute in a significant way to their goals and achievements. Activity by itself does not equal results.

If you can identify and eliminate the unproductive activities, you will free time to focus more on the few but crucial undertakings that are truly productive. The goal is to find both inefficiencies to eliminate and strengths you can make the most of. This process alone could double your effectiveness.

Being overwhelmed is often as unproductive as doing nothing and is far more unpleasant. Being selective, doing less but better, is a path to productivity. Focus on the important things and ignore the rest. Time is your friend, not your enemy, and there is plenty of it if you use it correctly.

Some big time wasters include activities you do only because other people ask you to do them; unproductive meetings, phone calls and conversations; reports that few people read; and things that have "always been done" but create little value. Eliminate as many of these activities as you can, or else get someone else to do them. You may need to be very creative to accomplish that. But once you implement this concept, your productivity will soar.

High Value Activities

It will take some time to identify the activities that contribute most to your results, but it is well worth the effort. Getting the truly important things done may not even require all of your time. Consider this: Where did the 8-to-5 culture come from? How is it possible that all the people in the world, regardless of the nature of their work, need exactly 8 hours to do it? An 80/20 manager does not operate like that.

Prior to having a severe retinal detachment, I was putting in eight-to-ten–hour days routinely, but after returning to work for half days only, I learned I could still get all my work done as long as I focused on the "vital few."

With thus rule in mind, your high value activities should include goal setting, hiring the right people, enriching employees' jobs, recognizing achievements, improving departmental work processes, fixing work environment problems, and other managerial duties to be discussed in this guide.

The most valuable tasks you do each day are often the hardest and most complex. But the rewards for completing them can be tremendous. So before you begin any activity, ask yourself, "Is this task in my "vital few" or "trivial many" category"?

Resist the temptation to clear up small things first. If you choose to start your day on low value tasks, you will spend the most productive time of the day on largely unimportant activities, and this is a habit you do not want to develop. Your ability to choose between what is really important and what is not will be a key determinant of your success. Effective, productive people discipline themselves to start on the most important task first. Teach your people to do the same and work steadily and single-mindedly until the project is completed.

80/20 In Your Personal Life

While the focus of this guide is on your work as manager, it is worth digressing briefly to point out that the 80/20 principle can also serve to enhance your personal life. If you can identify the most important people and activities in your life, the ones that lead to 80 percent of your happiness, and eliminate the "trivial many" you can free up time to have more fun and better relationships.

Management Types: Theory X vs. Theory Y

More than half a century ago Douglas McGregor wrote The Human Side of Enterprise (1960), in which he explained that people react to events based on their previous experiences, assumptions and beliefs. These factors define our behavior and, in turn, our behavior defines our attitude—not the other way around.

McGregor referred to the two opposing managerial beliefs and behaviors as "Theory X" and "Theory Y." Theory X managers assume the worst of their people: that they dislike work, do only the minimum amount necessary, have little desire to solve problems, avoid responsibility, need to be led and watched closely, and have little desire to achieve or advance within the organization. Given such beliefs, it makes sense that a Theory X manager feels people must be micromanaged!

Theory Y managers, however, rely on the exact opposite assumptions: that most people want to learn, do a good job, use their talents, accept responsibility, manage their own work, control their own fate, solve problems, make decisions, achieve positive results, be recognized for their good work, and grow within the organization.

The theory you believe in and practice is directly related to the results you will obtain from your employees. Your management style becomes a self-fulfilling prophecy. If you practice Theory X, as many managers still do, you will work with unhappy people who yield mediocre results. But if you practice Theory Y, more often than not your people will surprise you and will fulfill your positive expectations. They will be happy and productive when you give them the chance to do meaningful, challenging work and to achieve.

History of Theory X Management

Based on command and control, Theory X management was common in the past century- perhaps even justified when most work was physical, repetitive, or otherwise required little training and education. Management needed obedience and reliability first and foremost. Workers were told what was expected of them, and their job was to carry out instructions without asking questions

Today we live in a very different world. The market shifted from a manufacturing workforce to being information based, with skilled labor increasingly replaced physical labor. Rapid scientific and technical breakthroughs demand workers with more education and training. It is this kind of employees, with advanced technical, verbal and social skills, whom you manage today, and for whom a Theory X management style will backfire. Your people want and need to be trusted.

The Two-Factor Theory of Motivation

Early in my career I was introduced to a theory with tremendous application in the real world. Known as Herzberg's "Two-Factor Theory," it is one of the best management tools I have ever discovered. It changed my management life and it can do the same for you.

This theory, which addresses factors that lead to motivation and happiness in the workplace, was introduced by clinical psychologist Frederick Herzberg in his book *The Motivation to Work*, published in 1959. Later he developed it further in Work And the Nature Of Man, published in 1966. Also called the "Motivation–Hygiene theory," the concept is based on research in the field of job attitudes first conducted with engineers and accountants and then substantiated by at least 16 other investigations using a wide variety of populations.

Herzberg concluded that one set of job characteristics lead to employee satisfaction, and therefore motivation, while a completely separate and distinct set of job characteristics lead to employee dissatisfaction, and resulting unhappiness.

Factors that lead to employee satisfaction and motivation relate exclusively to the job itself—the work performed, as opposed to the work environment. These factors include achievement, recognition for achievements, the quality of the work to be performed (interesting and challenging), responsibility, advancement, and growth. When these factors are present in a job, the worker is likely to be happy and motivated, output increases, and turnover and absenteeism decrease.

Motivation is the unique human ability to experience psychological growth from our achievements. It is the hidden force within that causes us to take action, which in turn results in higher productivity. When people are truly motivated by the work they are doing, their own internal generators take over and they want to do the work. Most will seek more hours at work and are less likely to need outside stimulation.

Work environment factors (Herzberg called them hygiene factors) do not relate to the work itself but to factors such as company policies and administration, relationships with supervisors or other employees, salary, and other benefits. A problem with any one of these factors can be the cause of having many dissatisfied and unhappy employees. It is therefore important to identify and correct such problems as soon as you are aware of them. This should eliminate the dissatisfaction, but will not, by itself, motivate your workers.

Managers often confuse these two sets of factors, so they mistakenly try to manipulate work environment factors, such as work hours, days off, salary, bonuses, or other benefits to motivate people. This manipulation will not work because important work environment factors are not motivators. Salary, for example, may indeed motivate temporarily, but the effect soon wears off. Even a large raise will do you no good if you hate your job. That is the bottom line. You need to understand the difference between these two sets of factors in order to apply them correctly. Hygiene factors and motivational factors are discussed further in Chapters 3 and 5, respectively.

The Right Employees Are Your Greatest Asset

One of the best modern business books is Jim Collins' *Good to Great*, published in 2001. Collins studied 1,435 companies, focusing on 11 of them in different industries that went from good to great. He picked these companies based on stock price and the company's ability to sustain it for at least 15 years. To help determine why these companies were so successful, Collins compared each of them to a competitor in the same industry that remained mediocre.

Each great company had a CEO or leader who was a blend of humility and professionalism and had a strong desire to build a great company. These CEOs were modest and understated, as opposed to their competitors with big egos. CEO humility, it turned out, helped to build trust and allowed others to contribute without fear.

The other major finding that pertains to you directly, however, was that leaders who took companies from good to great focused first and foremost on placing the right people into the right jobs. Lacking that, all other efforts are futile. Therefore, one of your most important duties as a manager is to hire exceptional people into the right positions. The quality of your people is the backbone of a great department.

Collins concluded that with the right people in the right positions, other challenges, such as managing and motivating employees, require little effort. The right people are more likely to change direction more easily and are motivated by their inner drive to produce superior results. People are not your most important asset. The *right* people are! So look for character, basic intelligence and work ethic over specific knowledge and work experience. Most skills can be taught, but character cannot.

Chapter 1 Takeaway

- Keep the 80/20 rule in mind: 20 percent of inputs lead to 80 percent of results. Therefore find and focus on the "vital few" things that contribute most to your results and eliminate some of the "trivial many" that only waste time.
- Assume the best of your workers by implementing Theory Y as your management style.
- Distinguish between job-related factors that lead to job satisfaction and motivation, and environmental (hygiene) factors, which lead to dissatisfaction in the workplace.
- First and foremost, make sure to hire the right people for the right positions. All other advice will fail if this one is neglected.

Understand Your Real Job

O NE secret to being a successful manager is to know when to delegate instead of doing the work yourself. Handing the work to someone else frees your time to do tasks that are your responsibility rather than wasting it by performing work that skilled people on your staff can and should do.

If you manage a small department, you are a working manager and will be asked to handle some of the actual workload. But if you spend more time working rather than managing, this becomes a big problem.

As a manager you are judged on the success or failure of what your people do. Performance measures such as department productivity, for example, depend on everyone's combined efforts, not yours. Your job is to nurture and coach employees so they excel individually, but your success comes from their collective accomplishments. Because your success is so closely tied to theirs, you should do everything in your power to help them succeed.

Do Your Real Job

If you are a working manager, you are most likely very competent at doing the technical or professional work. In fact, you are probably better at it than anyone else, which is why you were promoted to manager in the first place. Furthermore, you like doing that work. Since training others is time consuming, it seems natural to keep on doing some or most of it yourself.

But that is not your job. Your *real* job is to perform the managerial duties that only you can do and leave the actual departmental work to people who were hired to do it. There is only so much time in the day. If you are so busy with non-managerial work, you may fall short in your managerial duties. You may even be so busy that you perceive questions from your employees as unwelcomed interruptions, which you should never do.

Moreover, by not delegating appropriate work to your employees, you are stifling their growth and development, minimizing their opportunities to achieve, lowering departmental productivity, and most importantly for you, taking time away from your real job as a manager.

Consider the Departmental Wheel

Think of your department as a wheel with you as the hub and each employee as a spoke. Your job is to make each spoke as strong as possible by hiring and developing exceptional people, then giving them meaningful and challenging jobs, providing them with necessary training and education, helping them set goals, coaching them, monitoring goals and performance, and making adjustments as necessary.

Think about it. If you maximize the effort and output of each person in your department, each spoke in the wheel will be solid. If you build a strong team who support one another and the department's goals, everyone will be moving in the same direction. You will have a successful department and be perceived as a successful manager. By focusing on everyone else, you are helping yourself. Develop your team and you will benefit as much as they do—probably even more.

Conversely, if your department wheel has weak spokes, it does not matter how hard you work. Your department will always be weak, and weak people will consume much of your time. They perform poorly, require careful watching, and inevitably require someone to clean up their shabby work. Furthermore, tolerating weak employees is unfair to your strong employees and impairs your ability to field a quality team. Low productivity workers cost you time and money both while they are on the job and while you spend valuable time replacing them.

Delegate All You Can

Your real job is to get the work done through others, which makes the job of delegating work a critical management skill. Unwillingness or inability to delegate is a leading cause of management failure. By delegating meaningful assignments that others are capable of doing, staff skills are further developed while your time is freed up for managerial duties.

Having a strong professional background helps you delegate properly by explaining the assignment comprehensively: why a task or project is needed and what results you expect. Delegating, therefore, also allows you to effectively coach throughout the assignment.

Conversely, a strong professional background will become a disadvantage if you continue to do the work yourself, if you micromanage after giving an assignment to someone else, or if you insist on having things done only your way.

If you are personally involved in any workflow, be sure to act quickly. Do not delay any work or decisions or else you will become the bottleneck.

What to Delegate

Delegate anything that is challenging, meaningful, and can help develop an employee's skills or enrich a job. Try not to do anything meaningful that someone else in the department can do, unless it is confidential or the work is intended exclusively for managers. Delegating meaningful work helps make another person's job challenging, eliminates frustration and resentment, reduces boredom, increases job satisfaction, and helps build self-esteem among your employees.

How to Delegate

Use your professional knowledge as an advantage. Clearly define the project, goals, deadlines, and your expectations. Explain why the work is being assigned and why it is important to the company or the client. Ask how the employee feels about the assignment and whether he or she needs new training. Then ask for a commitment.

People are more likely to commit to an assignment once they understand its importance and believe in it. Moreover, by fully understanding the assignment, people will be more creative in their approach to getting the work done.

Once you delegate a project, get out of the way. Make yourself available as a coach and consultant, but avoid micromanaging, which disrupts the process and causes employee frustration. Do not pull up the roots just to see how things are growing.

After you delegate and explain a major assignment, wait a few days and then ask the employee how things are progressing. See if any questions have come up since the project was assigned and ask about the project timeline. This will tell you how well the employee understood the assignment, whether he or she needs any clarification, and alerts you to signs of anxiety or confusion that could impede the desired results.

What Not to Delegate

Some duties cannot or should not be delegated. These you must do yourself as a manager. They include planning, preparing budgets, hiring, enriching jobs, setting goals, doing performance reviews, coaching employees, making staff development decisions, handling sensitive issues, and completing assignments requested by top management.

Also, avoid delegating an assignment to someone who is not good at it, or who does not like doing that type of work. Doing so will force people to be mediocre. Put people into positions where they enjoy their work and are good at it.

Chapter 2 Takeaway

- Your real job as manager is not to do the work, but to perform managerial duties and to coach and develop your staff.
- Your success is based on the output and success of the employees you manage. When they succeed, you succeed.
- You are the hub of the departmental wheel and your employees are the spokes. Develop each spoke to its full potential.
- Delegate everything you can that is meaningful and challenging. Clearly explain the assignment and its significance.
- Do not micromanage, but be readily available to coach.

CHAPTER 3

Managing the Work Environment

IN order to build mutual trust and get maximum productivity from your employees, you must truly believe they want to accept responsibility, manage their own work, solve their own problems, and work hard to achieve and succeed. It is from the way you act that they will know what you believe, and will respond accordingly. Remember what Emerson said: "What you are speaks so loudly that I can not hear what you say."

Because your real duty as a manager is to get the department work done through your employees, you must provide them with two key things:

1. A good work environment

2. Jobs that motivate

This chapter will focus on the first task: creating a positive workplace environment. Chapters 4 and 5 will explore means to motivate your workers.

As manager, you should continuously monitor the work-place, being on the lookout for problems that are causing significant dissatisfaction and unhappiness. By talking to your employees individually and at meetings, you should be able to uncover any significant problems. Keep in mind that one problem alone may be disturbing one or several employees.

Identify and rectify "hygiene problems," but do not spend too much time on them. Keep it simple. Just make changes, try to be fair and equitable, do not make a big deal out of the problem, and move on. Spend more of your time on two of your most important tasks: job enrichment and creating real motivation, which are covered in Chapters 4 and 5, respectively.

Managing the Most Frequent Workplace Problems

Below are the workplace problems that Herzberg's research identified as the ones that most frequently cause dissatisfaction (unhappiness) among your workers and advice on how to successfully address them.

1. Company Policy and Administration

Every company has some outdated or unnecessary policies, burdensome paperwork, or rules and regulations that frustrate employees. As manager, you should identify and correct as many of these as you can. If you schedule regular discussions both with individuals and through departmental meetings, you should be able to identify rules, policies and procedures that employees strongly dislike. Then make changes if you can. Some policies or rules may be easy to improve, change or even eliminate, without any negative effect on the company or department.

2. Supervision and Relationship with the Supervisor

Nothing causes more frustration for employees than a bad relationship with their immediate supervisor. Just one bad supervisor can cause extreme unhappiness among several members of a department.

Studies have shown that 70 percent of the people who quit their job do so because of their immediate boss/supervisor. The guilty supervisor may not realize that, however, because disguised exit interview studies have shown that most employees do not wish to burn bridges; as a result, they will not name their supervisor as the primary reason for leaving their jobs.

Supervisors who cause the most stress typically have a Theory X management style, or exhibit some behaviors associated with it. They are prone to yelling, threatening, or micromanaging and are not open to new ideas or suggestions. It is imperative that you not be one of them, but instead build trust with each employee in your department.

As department manager, you are being evaluated by your employees every time you have contact with them. Your people are measuring everything you say and do, and they are wondering whether you are for or against them. Like it or not, this scrutiny automatically comes with the power given to you as manager.

If you fail to greet an employee on a bad day, for instance, the interpretation will be, "I must have done something wrong." Each worker observes your actions keenly and draws his or her own conclusions about its meaning. As employees begin to trust you and see you are on their side, the scrutiny and fear will subside, but it never goes away completely.

Years ago, when I was a product manager, I had a temporary assistant who after a couple weeks told me, "you're not as big of an SOB as everyone said you were." I was shocked. She explained that when I walked down the hall I never acknowledged employees sitting at their desks. And when I asked for refreshments at meetings, I was not friendly enough in the way I phrased my request. (Back in those days we still had secretaries who did these things.)

That day I learned that I was being judged at all times, especially by the people who reported to me or who were lower in the corporate hierarchy. I learned how important it was to acknowledge people at all times, no matter how focused I might have been on anything else. It was a valuable lesson.

People want a boss/supervisor they can respect, learn from, and with whom they feel comfortable speaking openly. Mutual respect comes when they know their work is appreciated, when they are treated fairly, and when they know they can speak candidly with their supervisor without negative repercussions. In turn, they will then listen to you. This is the relationship you should strive for.

Give clear directions and then let the employee figure out how to do the job. If they trust you, they will feel safe coming to you for help when needed.

If you have a concern about any of your employees, or you sense they have a problem with you, meet with them privately, preferably in their office. Make sure to ask them to talk about the problem first. Then, after listening to their side, present your viewpoint and let them respond. Then determine how to resolve the problem together.

3. Workplace and Work Conditions

The physical environment of concern to your employees includes building location, office size and location, furniture and equipment, noise levels, even office temperature.

Your ability to change work conditions may be limited. Just be fair and equitable and do your best to provide an environment that fits the needs of the worker and the type of work being done as much as possible and within your budget. But always keep in mind that resolving a work condition problem will eliminate the dissatisfaction but will not, by itself, serve to motivate employees.

4. Interpersonal Relationships

Having positive relationships with colleagues, either with peers or with those in the hierarchy chain, is naturally a key factor in employees' perception of their workplace environment. Inevitably, conflicts will occur at times. When they get serious, you, as manager, must step in to get employees to resolve their conflict. Meet alone with each person. Then, after you understand the issue from each point of view, bring them together to discuss the problem and agree on a solution.

To help prevent or minimize conflicts, try to hire people who seem to work well with others, although you will never know for sure before you hire them. Allowing other department members to interact with job candidates during the hiring process will help you hire compatible people.

The desire for good interpersonal relationships is closely related to the "social need," as discussed in Abraham H. Maslow's

"Hierarchy of Needs." His theory is that human needs are organized hierarchically, and when one need is satisfied, the next level need takes over.

More often than not, professional workers today make adequate salaries and benefits, so their lower-level needs for survival (food and shelter), plus safety and security, are fairly well satisfied. Therefore, the next level—social need—moves to the top. People wish to be accepted by their peers and feel they are an integral part of the group.

You can help your employees fill their social need by holding departmental events such as birthdays, lunches, and holiday outings. These social gatherings help employees get to know each other in a casual, stress-free environment, build cohesiveness, and help everyone feel part of the group.

5. Salary

What makes salary so interesting is that it is often misused in an attempt to motivate people. A common source of dissatisfaction is compensation inequality, when salaries are perceived to be significantly lower than those of others doing similar jobs in similar organizations. When the budget permits, you should offer salaries and raises that reduce or eliminate employee dissatisfaction and rectify inequities. In special cases, you may use raises to keep an excellent employee from leaving.

But managers often give raises for the wrong reasons—sometimes in the hope it will improve employee performance. That makes no sense when you consider money, by itself, is not a motivator. Salaries need to be fair and equitable, or else people will be dissatisfied. But simply throwing more money at them beyond the point perceived as equitable, is a waste of money, and does not motivate.

Except for a very short period of time, people are never completely satisfied with their salary or bonus and will always want more. Some will frequently look for new jobs that pay more. The best thing you can do is to pay an equitable salary while providing great jobs with plenty of responsibility, purpose, autonomy, and opportunities to learn and achieve.

Again, just keep compensation simple, fair and equitable and pay enough so people can focus on their work and not on their salary. A one-time, performance-based surprise bonus is a good way to use money as a reward. While it links money to performance, it does not set a new salary level or a new level of bonus expectations.

Be careful with expectations regarding salary and bonuses. Research indicates that a salary bump does increase happiness for about six months. But in the long run, that salary increase creates future expectations that may not be realistic. If an employee receives a $1,000 salary increase one year, but only $500 the next year, he will be disappointed because, psychologically, he is taking a $500 cut in his raise. After the first raise, the baseline expectation for the next raise became $1,000.

Annual bonuses have a similar effect. A bonus smaller than the one received the previous year creates disappointment. And you can be sure that almost everyone looks back to see what they received the previous year.

I cannot stress this enough because I know it is something difficult for many people to believe: money is *not* a motivator, as demonstrated in Herzberg's research and other studies thereafter. If not administered properly, salary increases and bonuses can actually backfire. Do not spend a lot of time on compensation, but be sure it is fair and equitable to prevent resentment.

Spend most of your time on work-related motivational factors (see Chapter 5). They are the things that will bring employees satisfaction and happiness, and will motivate them toward peak performance.

A recent trend in some large companies, especially the tech companies in California's Silicon Valley, is to provide employees with free benefits such as food, shuttle buses, gymnasiums, ice cream parlors, and even dry cleaning services. These extra perks are supposed to make the life of a busy employee easier, keep them onsite during the day, and promote contact with other employees.

The cost of these perks may be worthwhile if they extend work hours and if they help fill the social need. But they cost money and are not motivators Most likely, this money would be better spent on things that relate to the job itself, such as education and training.

These new perks may help entice new employees to join a company rather than the competition when the jobs and compensation are comparable. For this reason you may have to add some of these perks to compete for new hires. But ultimately, all companies are in effect spending more money without actually succeeding in motivating employees.

Some companies promote flexibility by allowing people to work from home. But increasingly companies are requiring their workers to spend more time in the office because they believe interaction encourages innovation and creativity. Studies seem to confirm that people who work at home are less innovative, but they are also more productive. So you need to decide what is most important to you.

6. Status

Status, a person's perception of his or her standing or importance in the company, is a less frequently mentioned "hygiene" factor, but a very important one because it helps build self-worth and self-confidence. Here are a few things you can do to give your people a sense of enhanced status.

Give credit where credit is due

As the manager, you can help build the perception of status by always giving employees full credit for their work and achievements. Never grab credit for yourself because it diminishes the employees' perception of their status and destroys trust. Stealing credit is the sign of a weak, insecure manager.

Also, if multiple people have contributed to a project, be sure to mention the name of each person and be specific about their contributions. This serves to help build their self-esteem and status.

Encourage employees to make presentations

Encourage your people to make company presentations whenever it makes sense, but do not force them to do so. This shows you trust them, enhances their status within the company, and helps develop their presentation skills. If you are unsure about how well the employee can present, ask him or her to practice the talk and then present it to you before presenting it to others.

Many managers grab the glory for themselves by making most departmental presentations, instead of deferring the privilege to those who do the actual work. Some of these managers may do this because of their egos, but some may they think this is their responsibility as department head. Whatever the reason, they are missing a great opportunity to build trust and to enhance the employee's feelings of heightened status.

Share information with your people

As manager, you will be privy to a plethora of corporate and departmental information. While some of it is confidential, most is not. When you hear any interesting, non-confidential information about the company, write it down and share it with your people at the next department meeting. This helps build their feelings of status and security and builds mutual trust.

Often, managers are so busy that they forget to keep their people informed. Because much of the information available to you as manager is not pertinent to a workers' actual job, it may not occur to you to pass it on. But your employees like to be in the loop, and the more you tell them about what is going on in the company, the better they will feel about their position in it.

At times I used to hold departmental meetings where some people, including the administrative staff, were excluded because their work was not directly related to the information I shared with others. I just assumed they would not be interested. I learned this was a big mistake when a staff member told me how disappointed she was that she was not invited.

You cannot always invite everyone to meetings where information is shared, but people wish so much to be "in on things" that you should consider carefully whom you exclude from a meeting, and possibly consider alternate ways of passing that information on to them.

Work Environment Needs Do Not Change

A compilation of findings from more recent studies about what workers consider especially important in today's work environment is consistent with Herzberg's Two-Factor Theory. Human nature, after all, does not change. The workers of today are concerned about the same issues as half a century ago.

They want a supervisor who treats them fairly and like adults, whom they can respect and learn from, who keeps them informed, listens, keeps commitments, and who supports them when needed. They want clear direction on their job, but once they have that, workers clearly desire the autonomy to figure out how to do their job on their own. They want a supervisor who trusts them to get the work done without being a micromanager, but who is willing to listen and coach them when they ask for help.

Workers want an environment that fits their needs and people they enjoy working with. They want a worthwhile job and a company that has a worthwhile core purpose they can get excited about. Note that salary and benefits are not mentioned among things workers want most.

Chapter 3 Takeaway

- Workplace ("hygiene") problems cause dissatisfaction; correcting them reduces dissatisfaction and unhappiness, but does not improve motivation.
- Eliminate unnecessary policies and burdensome paperwork whenever possible.
- Supervisory issues can be a major problem. Practice Theory-Y-style management.
- Remember that employees are always watching your actions, which speak far louder than your words.
- Watch for signs of interpersonal problems and help fix them when you can.
- Compensation becomes an issue if employees perceive it to be inequitable compared to that of others holding similar jobs. Make sure salaries and bonus distributions are fair and equitable, but do not try to use them as motivators.
- Work constantly to enhance the feeling of status among your employees.

Enriching Jobs

Job enrichment, also known as job redesign, is the key to creating more motivated employees and to solving most motivation problems. It is important because worker motivation is derived from the actual job they do.

Job enrichment is not job enlargement. The latter happens when you add additional routine activities to an already unpleasant job. Job enrichment, by contrast, seeks to broaden the scope of a job, creates a more complete job, adds more responsibility, and allows employees more autonomy to get their jobs done.

The process of job enrichment results in jobs that provide more opportunities to achieve. This in turn allows employees to experience the ensuing motivation. And more achievements give managers and colleagues more chances to recognize those achievements, again enhancing motivation.

Components of an Enriched Job

Your most important duty as a manager is to hire the right people into the right positions. The next most important duty, however, is for you to design meaningful, enriched jobs that give each employee significant responsibility and opportunities for achievement. Here are the three most important attributes of an enriched job:

A Complete Job

As much as possible, give each employee responsibility for a complete job (all the pieces) that results in a definable product or service. When the job is done, the worker should be able to see a real change in the product or service.

Building a complete job streamlines workflow and improves efficiency. When tasks done by separate people or departments are combined into one job, bottlenecks and delays are reduced or eliminated. Consolidating multiple tasks into one job increases responsibility, a strong motivator for most people.

Decision-Making Control

Employees should have as much control as possible over how they complete their work, as long as it is done right and on time. Competent employees should be allowed to schedule their own work, deviate from normal procedures in unusual situations, and have real authority and responsibility for cost and budget control.

Direct Feedback on How the Job Is Being Done

Ideally, each employee should get direct feedback from the internal or external customer/client on how well they perform and on any problems that occur. Preferably, feedback should come directly from the customer and not through the supervisor.

Depending on the type of work done in your department, it may be possible to assign an employee or small team responsibility for all the work for a specific customer. This facilitates direct communication between worker and customer. If there is a problem, the employee gets an opportunity to fix it before the boss intervenes.

All Three Components Are Important

All three dimensions of an enriched job discussed above are important and interrelated. For example, when a job is incomplete (fractionated) and the employee does only part of the work, he or she feels little ownership. This makes it difficult to allow the person significant decision-making. Positive feedback means little to a worker who has completed only part of the job or had little input in the process of doing the job.

Creating more complete jobs, without giving control, does little to enrich the job or to improve motivation.

The Job Enrichment Process

Enriching individual jobs requires that you first examine the overall workflow and processes within your department. Developing a streamlined departmental workflow, with improved efficiency, makes it easier for you to enrich individual jobs. Below are the steps to workflow evaluation and job enrichment.

1. Analyze Department Workflow/Processes

Develop flowcharts and analyze the type and volume of important department work tasks and their time requirements. To help you see the big picture, use the responsibility tables (see Chapter 9) that you should have for each employee.

2. Analyze Related Tasks Inside and Outside the Department

Determine if any important tasks now being done outside your department could be done inside your department. Conversely, identify any tasks now done inside your department that don't fit departmental workflow and could be done by someone outside your department. Look carefully to determine if any tasks or responsibilities contribute little, and can be eliminated altogether, according to the 80/20 rule.

3. Reorganize Workflow/Processes if Needed

If your workflow is logical and efficient, leave it alone. But most likely it can be streamlined and improved. Depending on the type and volume of major tasks, and the clients for whom they are being done, you may end up dividing your department into multiple work units. Evaluate the advantages and disadvantages of having individuals in your department perform all the work for specific customers.

4. Evaluate Each Employee

Review the skills, training and education of the employees whose jobs you are enriching, so you fully understand their capabilities. Meet with them to discuss current responsibilities, using the responsibility table as a guide. Discuss what type of work and specific tasks they like doing, what they do not like, and what other jobs they would like to do in the future. This gives you a good idea of the employees capabilities, current responsibilities, what they like doing, and their future aspirations.

5. Enrich the Job

Based on employee information and overall department workflow and processes, redesign the individual job by combining tasks and adding responsibilities to make the job more complete and less fragmented. As much as possible, assigned tasks should fit together logically, so the employee is responsible for a complete job. If it cannot be a whole job for one person, make it a whole job for a team.

If it makes sense, give the employee responsibility for doing all the work for a specific customer. If you can do this, then establish a direct feedback link so, when problems arise, they go from the customer to the employee first. Check periodically with customers to be sure they are completely satisfied.

Give the employee as much autonomy as possible for getting the job done, including planning, timing, and monitoring progress and budgets.

Sometimes, if workers are doing something they dislike, it is best to just give that task to someone who does not mind doing it. Focus on getting the job done while trying to design jobs around each person's strengths.

Evaluate the Need for Training

By enriching jobs you are adding responsibility and giving workers more autonomy in planning and completing their work. You must evaluate whether more training is needed, and provide it so the worker can be successful in the new, enriched job.

Potential Job Enrichment Concerns

With job enrichment, you will be making changes that may scare some people, so be sure to discuss what you are trying to do, and why.

Explain to the employee how the new job will be more complete, give him more responsibility, more autonomy, and more direct feedback from the customer. Be sure to discuss any training that you or the employee think is needed, and decide how to provide it.

Most workers will welcome an enriched job with more responsibility and autonomy; but some may not. After discussing it with them, if a worker does not want to accept the new responsibilities, you must address the situation. Perhaps you can switch some responsibilities between employees, or move the unhappy employee into another job within the department. If the reluctance persists, however, you should help move the person into another department or out of the company. Remember, you must get the right people into the right positions within your department.

Chapter 4 Takeaway

- Job *enlargement* simply adds more routine activities to an already unpleasant job. Nobody wants that.
- Job *enrichment* broadens the scope of a job and adds responsibility, thereby providing more opportunities to achieve. It is the starting point for employee motivation.
- Key characteristics of an enriched job are its wholeness, employee autonomy, and direct feedback from the customer.
- Continually monitor department workflow and tasks to help enrich all department positions over time.
- Job enrichment can be threatening; make sure your employee understands what you are doing and why, and seek their input.

Managing Motivation

THE best way to motivate your people is by allowing them to perform work commensurate with their abilities. When that happens, achievement and recognition follow. Motivated people have the internal desire and willingness to do their job and, consequently, deliver a higher level of output and productivity—exactly what you want as a manager.

Motivation comes from doing meaningful, challenging and important work that allows employees to use their education, training and skills. The process of job enrichment helps you create good jobs, which are motivating and satisfying because they give employees opportunities to achieve and, in turn, to be recognized for those achievements.

Reasons for Poor Motivation

A person's attitude and level of motivation is usually appropriate for the job being done. If the job offers little opportunity to achieve something meaningful, it is hard for that person not to suffer from poor motivation and a bad attitude. Here are the three primary reasons for a worker's poor motivation at work.

1. A Bad Job

Uninteresting jobs that fail to challenge and offer little opportunity to achieve something meaningful often result in poorly motivated employees. Luckily, you probably manage technical or professional workers with substantial education and training, so their work should already be at least somewhat challenging and meaningful. If not, they are underutilized and probably demotivated. With a little thought and effort, you can improve these jobs through job enrichment.

Talent stripped of the opportunity to achieve results in boredom and frustration. Quality employees will leave sooner or later if they are not challenged to their potential and allowed to achieve something meaningful. This is especially true of young workers today who look for jobs where they can both learn and make a difference.

Highly specialized or fragmented jobs, in which workers use only a few skills and are responsible for only a portion of the work, can become monotonous, resulting in boredom, frustration, low motivation, lower productivity, absenteeism, and turnover. Again, the solution here is job enrichment.

2. A Bad Boss

Recent studies indicate that about 40 percent of U.S. workers believe they work for a bad supervisor. The most frequent complaints are that managers fail to keep promises, do not give credit where credit is due, give employees the silent treatment, make negative comments, invade their privacy, and blame others for their mistakes. To make it even worse, bad managers are often oblivious to the negative impact they have on their employees.

Authoritarian, Theory-X managers, and other bad supervisors do not understand the frustration that comes from micromanagement and excess control. When workers' discretion and control over their jobs are minimized, the result is apathy and demotivation. Conversely, when given more control, a complete job, and decision-making power over their own work, motivation is enhanced and problems tend to disappear.

Bad supervisors also fail to identify and acknowledge employee achievement. In so doing, they overlook the fact that personal recognition is a major motivational factor and therefore miss out on opportunities to motivate.

Many supervisors wrongly believe that performance will improve if they can improve a worker's attitude, which they try to change by using artificial motivators, such as pep talks, goal discussions, even contests. But these attempts usually fail because manipulation of work-environment factors does not motivate. To change a worker's behavior and attitude you must first give that person a good job to do.

3. Inability to Do the Job/Lack of Training

A motivational problem may exist because an employee is not properly trained or technically competent to do the job, which results in frustration for that person and inability to succeed in their work.

If someone is not performing satisfactorily, first look at the job itself to see if it needs to be enriched. If the job is good, determine if the worker is properly trained. If not, provide the training and education necessary for this specific job. These are major motivators because they help employees do their jobs properly and, therefore, to achieve.

Best Ways to Support Motivation

Although motivation comes mostly from within, there are ways in which you can significantly enhance the motivation of your staff. Herzberg's Two-Factor Theory explains how achievement, recognition, the work itself, and responsibility are the four strongest motivators leading to extreme satisfaction at work. Advancement and personal growth are also strong motivators but occur less frequently. Here are the best ways for you to help motivate your staff, according to Herzberg.

1. Achievement

Achievement is the positive feeling a person experiences after doing something well. Even small achievements can motivate a worker to try to improve on their performance.

The number of opportunities for an employee to achieve something meaningful, and the resulting motivation, will depend on the job you design for that person through your job enrichment efforts.

During my career I worked in many areas, including marketing research, product management, licensing, business development, and strategic planning. I liked marketing research best because it gave me the most opportunities for achievement. Every report and every product evaluation, positive or negative, was an achievement. By comparison, achievement in licensing is rare. In one year I evaluated over one hundred in-licensing opportunities without closing one deal. No deal meant no achievement, and lack of achievement meant no recognition and lots of frustration.

As a manager, it is very important that you spend significant time on job enrichment so you can provide your employees with jobs that give them multiple opportunities to achieve.

2. Recognition for Achievements

After you enrich a job to the point where an employee is able to achieve, the next best thing you can do is to identify those meaningful achievements when they happen, and then find a way to recognize them: in person, by phone, via a note, or e-mail. No cost, high reward!

Recognition for achievement was the second most frequently mentioned motivator in the Herzberg studies, right after achievement itself. People desire the positive feelings that come from being recognized for their successful work, but recognition can only happen if others are made aware of their accomplishments and, in turn, recognize them for their good work. As manager, it is up to you to recognize the achievements of your employees. If you don't, who will?

Words of praise for any achievement are recognition. Watch for achievements, and then recognize the accomplishment as soon as possible, publicly or privately.

We know that the main reason people leave their jobs is their immediate supervisor, but a recent survey found that the more specific reason was limited praise and recognition from the supervisor. This finding reinforces how important praise and recognition are, and why every manager with an understanding of motivation should look out for achievements to recognize.

Managers want to increase motivation and productivity, so why do they not spend more time seeking out and recognizing achievements? Probably because they fail to understand that recognition can motivate workers and build self-esteem, and they are oblivious to the motivational influences of these actions. Some managers think they do not have time to seek out achievements, even though they want more productivity—and recognition is one of the best ways to get it.

Based on my 42 years of industry experience, I can tell you that getting recognized for an achievement is rare. Managers rarely give kudos. If your supervisor does, consider yourself very lucky. By finding and recognizing achievements you will set yourself apart from most other managers.

Finally, some managers fail to recognize achievements because they think money is the only form of recognition. They do not realize that words like "thank you, I appreciate your effort in getting this to me so quickly," or "I could never do it that well" are the best forms of recognition.

In 1978, I was hired to establish a market research department in a small cardiovascular pharmaceutical company. An important part of my job was to evaluate the marketability of drugs in our R&D pipeline. After a year on the job I was called into the office of my supervisor, the vice president of marketing and sales. He presented me with a letter from the company president saying that I was one of the few people singled out as having made an exceptional contribution to our division and to receive a discretionary bonus. The letter included comments from my supervisor about my achievements.

Did I keep this letter? Hell yes, I'm holding onto it right now, 34 years later. I still remember how great I felt that day. I was flying high and could not wait to tell my wife. The money was nice, but the recognition for my achievements was far better. This company knew how to recognize and to motivate people, and I still consider it the best company I ever worked for.

Take the opportunity to recognize achievement every chance you get. Force yourself to do this—most managers do not. When you are in the mindset of looking for positive things people are doing, it is easy to find them. Catch people doing something well—doing exceptional work, giving a speech or presentation, helping someone else, or writing a great report. Pull them aside and tell them, in specific terms, what they did and why it was so good. Praise often and be specific.

While you should always praise people for their behavior and achievements, never praise them on how they look or dress, because this can be misinterpreted and land you in trouble. Be as specific as possible in linking your praise to people's work. Also, do not praise routine work, because it will come off as insincere and phony.

Never set up competition by comparing employees. For example, saying something like "you are the best analyst in the department" will make others appear to be rivals rather than collaborators. If someone is improving on a bad habit—perhaps being late for work less often, or missing fewer deadlines—consider it an achievement. Recognize improvement as well, not just absolute achievements.

Motivated employees are satisfied, happy employees. They are absent less, more productive and less likely to leave the job. Recognizing achievements costs you nothing, but will pay you back royally.

Finding and recognizing achievement

Here are some ideas to help you identify and recognize achievements:

- Get into a mindset of looking for achievements every day.
- List and use several ways you can show appreciation.
- Spend more time with your staff to discover achievement when it happens.
- Give recognition for an achievement soon after you identify it.
- For those who need improvement, recognize even small achievements.
- Using a list of employees, put an X beside anyone who achieves something meaningful. Circle each X after you have recognized that achievement.

At my last company the director of business development, who reported to me, was responsible for writing proposals and nurturing prospective clients until a contract was signed. She hired an assistant who previously worked at our company as a project manager and was able to hit the road running. This new employee wrote several proposals during her first two months on the job, and her performance exceeded our expectations.

The director and I called this new employee into an office, sat her down, and told her we thought she was doing a terrific job, and why. How do you think she felt? Motivated? This cost us nothing except a few minutes of our time.

How people feel about you will depend on how you make them feel. So go looking for achievements by your workers and colleagues. Yes, I added colleagues. Everyone wants to be recognized, even those who say they do not care—even top management. Give a speech or presentation and let someone tell you how good it was. See how you feel. Recognize others every chance you get. It makes people feel great, and when this happens they will feel good about you as well. And good interpersonal relationships enhance cooperation when you need it most.

3. The Work Itself

The third most-frequently-mentioned motivational factor in Herzberg's studies, the work itself, is closely related to the achievement factor. People want meaningful work that provides them ample opportunities to achieve.

And again, the best way to do this is through job enrichment, as discussed in Chapter 4. This process is the real generator for employee motivation, job satisfaction and happiness.

Without a good job, a worker cannot experience the other motivational factors discussed in this chapter. He will not have much responsibility or opportunity to achieve, and without achievements he will not receive recognition. Chances for advancement and growth will be poor. How can he be happy?

Creating challenging and meaningful jobs that offer opportunities to achieve may be your single most important management responsibility, second only to hiring great people.

4. Responsibility

Responsibility is a motivational factor mentioned almost as frequently as the work itself. Employees want real responsibility and control over their work. Give them as much responsibility and authority as possible, and be sure this is well defined in the job description and list of responsibilities. These three factors—responsibility, the work itself, and achievement–all are closely related. A good job will offer plenty of responsibility and opportunities to achieve.

You can add responsibility to a job by removing some controls, giving additional authority, increasing personal accountability, assigning a complete unit of work, or assigning employees to a specific areas in which they can acquire expertise.

Through job enrichment you will be adding responsibility, consolidating tasks, reducing fragmentation, making jobs more complete, and giving employees more control over their own work. The work itself (job content) is improved. Over time, as your workers develop their skills, give them more responsibility whenever possible.

5. Advancement

Advancement (promotion) happens less frequently but is an important motivational factor. Each worker will be handled differently, depending on performance and positions available in your department and company. In some cases a promotion must wait until a position becomes available. In others, you may be able to promote a person into a better title even though the actual work remains the same.

Promotions require a delicate balance. Consider your best performers carefully. If you think a promotion is necessary to retain one of them, you may need to enhance his or her title along with a small increase in salary.

6. Growth

Growth is another important motivational factor. People want job growth, which can mean many things. Most employees, particularly young people, want to learn more about their job and their company. Some want to acquire new skills, or build status and self-esteem. As manager, you should provide growth opportunities provided they makes sense for the employee, the department, and the company.

If training or education can improve employee performance within the current job, or prepare the person for a better job within the company, than it is probably justified. However, paying for training and education unrelated to the job itself is not a wise use of company money, and you should deny unjustified requests.

Conferences and tradeshows

Be careful with conferences and tradeshows. Often they are boondoggles where attendees mainly visit with old classmates and friends. Be sure any request to attend is a justifiable use of money. Each attendee should have a good rationale and a personal goal for attending. Ask them to write a report or do a presentation afterward.

I've observed many conferences and tradeshows where company attendees do very little and gain very little. Some view attendance as a perk or reward. Not only is the trip itself a waste of company money, but any productive work the employee could have been doing on the job during that time is wasted money as well.

People Have Not Changed Over the Decades

More recent studies on "what workers want" support what experts like Hertzberg had already found to be the main motivators long ago: Interesting, exciting work, satisfaction from doing something important, and praise from a supervisor who appreciates them.

Chapter 5 Takeaway

- If you see poor motivation among your workers, check first for the following culprits: a bad job, a bad supervisor, or insufficient training.
- Achievement is the primary motivator, so provide enriched jobs that give employees significant opportunities to achieve.
- Recognition for achievement is another strong motivator. Seek out and recognize accomplishments.
- The work itself is a crucial motivator, closely related to achievement. Design challenging, meaningful jobs that offer plenty of opportunities to achieve.
- Responsibility is a strong motivator. Give your employees as much responsibility and autonomy as possible.
- Advancement and growth are less frequent but also important motivators.

CHAPTER 6

Department Management

TRADITIONAL management textbooks divide management into the following four broad categories:

Planning: Deciding what must be done; developing goals and action plans to achieve it; budgeting and forecasting.

Organizing: Separating work functions; deciding what resources are needed to perform each function, which positions will be responsible for performing each job, and staffing those positions.

Influencing: Formerly known as "directing"—an older term used for autocratic managers who barked orders like cops on TV shows; influencing suggests a more collaborative process, which includes means to motivate the staff to get the work done.

Controlling (monitoring): This function includes the use of feedback, quantitative reports, and update meetings to monitor progress and ensure plans are on track, the work is being done correctly, and goals are being met.

Planning

As department manager, you should be required by your company to provide an annual departmental plan with goals. If not, write one for your own good anyway. Without a plan, you will stumble without clear direction as to where you are headed; and without goals, you will have difficulty knowing what decisions and expenditures should be made.

Most likely upper management will provide corporate goals that you must support. They may assign some departmental goals they think you should meet. If you believe these goals are unreasonable, develop some good arguments and attempt to get them changed for everyone's good.

Goals are the backbone of your plan and are further discussed below. Departmental tasks, expenditures, personnel, supplies and equipment in your plan should all link back to your goals, because these are the things needed to reach your goals.

Any expenditure that does not contribute to your goals or to some significant improvement in your department should be questioned. In the real world, annual plans are usually tied to budgets and are negotiated with upper management. You want more budget dollars and they want to cut you back. I learned this the hard way: ask for a little more then you need because management will most likely cut you back no matter what you request. Depending on the type of work done in your department, you may be asked to forecast revenue, units produced or sold, or some other quantitative or qualitative output. To do this, look back at historical numbers and current trends, consider your company's future business strategies, and use good common sense.

Spend a good portion of your time on planning because it sets the direction for your department. It is your roadmap for future decisions. Finally, involve your key people in the planning process. Without their involvement, it will be difficult to get their commitment. Furthermore, including your people in this process will help generate new ideas.

Goal Setting

Research shows that only about three percent of people have clearly written goals, but they accomplish ten times more than others with equal education who do not have written goals. An average person with clearly written goals and the ability to get important tasks done efficiently will run circles around a genius with no written goals.

A national survey of 300 small businesses showed that over 80 percent of those who had goals did not keep track of them, and 77 percent had yet to achieve their goals.

Your ability to set goals around the most important responsibilities in your department and to get work started and completed in a timely manner, will have significant impact on your success as a manager. Successful people launch directly into their top priority tasks and have the discipline to work steadily until they are completed. Once your goals are written down and met you will know whether your department has succeeded in doing what it is supposed to do and what is expected from upper management.

Staff Participation in Goal Setting

Develop your departmental goals as soon as you know what work output is required from your department, including what is needed to support corporate goals. Be sure to include key members of your staff who will be involved in doing the work. By including them, you are more likely to get commitment and avoid complaints that occur when goals are dictated without input from those who actually do the work. Goal setting should also include discussions of possible problems, as well as resources needed to reach each goal.

Performance will be affected by the person who sets the goals and by the employees' perception of what is reasonable. Goals set by the department manager without input from those doing the work are likely to be problematic.

If the goals are perceived to be reasonable, results will tend to be satisfactory. Goals should be specific, measurable, stretch but reachable, and time specific. Once goals are set, communicate them clearly in writing to all department members as well as your supervisor.

Organizing

Just because the responsibilities and workflow of your department are already established does not mean they are optimized for maximum efficiency. Make sure to take a close look at each departmental task and responsibility in an 80/20 fashion to determine what is really important and what could be streamlined or eliminated. Evaluate each work segment to determine if it is of high value. If not, find a way to stop doing this work, minimize the time spent on it, or else pass it on to another department that should be doing it. As much as possible, eliminate activities that contribute very little to departmental results.

Once you identify high-value activities and understand the strength of your people, you should be able to organize the work efficiently to best meet departmental goals. While doing this, be sure to enrich as many jobs as possible by making them more complete and giving employees more autonomy and control over their own work.

Staffing

Staffing is an important segment of the organizing function. It includes determining the qualifications necessary to fill each position and whether you have the right person in each position. Hiring is discussed separately in Chapter 8.

As previously discussed, a good manager understands the importance of having the right people in the right positions. Start by doing an assessment of your current staff. If you are new to management, it will take some time to learn about each person's strengths, weaknesses, capabilities and contributions. Do they have the right training and skills to do their jobs? Do they enjoy their work and do they get it done on time while maintaining a high standard of quality?

Once you determine that, privately rank the value of each department member on an A-F scale. Include a list of what you like and dislike, and the strengths and weaknesses you see in each person. This information will be very useful when you embark on the job enrichment process.

Next, develop an action plan for each person who needs training, coaching, or movement out of the department. Work on bringing lower-rated people to the A-B (top 20 percent) level. If this turns out to be impossible, replace them over time.

Identify the top-20-percent, A-B-rated workers who you definitely want to keep. Do whatever it takes to keep them. Spend sufficient time with them to make sure they are happy and that their jobs are as challenging, meaningful, and enriched as possible.

Most likely, the less productive bottom 50 percent of the people in your department consume a disproportionate amount of your time and energy while contributing far less. Keep this in mind so you can spend more of your time nurturing your best employees. Do not let your top people feel underappreciated or taken for granted. Show them your appreciation by enhancing their jobs and recognizing their accomplishments. Help your winners grow and succeed rather than waste time trying to salvage those who should not be in your department.

Try to match people with work they like and are good at doing. Do not force anyone to do a job they dislike. Matching workers with jobs will take time and serious discussions with each employee, but it is well worth the effort. Once your people are doing what they enjoy and are good at, they will be happier, more motivated, and more productive.

You must remove those who are a poor match for the positions they hold. This can be difficult, but without great people you cannot have a great department. If someone does not fit in and does not respond to coaching and training, the person needs to be replaced.

It is not wrong to lay off people who threaten the productivity and motivation of your department. If anything, it is unfair to leave these people in the dark about their weaknesses and allow them to stay in jobs where they are failing. Do not delay the firing, but be humane. Give them time off to look for another job, but set deadlines. Also, make sure you have good documentation and work closely with your human resources (HR) department. And consider that you may be doing them a favor. People who do a poor job are probably a bad fit and will be much happier after they find a job better suited to their needs and capabilities.

Monitoring Feedback

Monitoring, also known as control, is part of your managerial responsibilities. It involves obtaining updates from your employees and from relevant quantitative reports from the finance and other pertinent company departments. This information is necessary for you to know how well your people are progressing toward individual and departmental goals. When you see problems, you can discuss them with your staff and make changes to get back on track. As a Theory Y manager, be sure to do the monitoring in a subtle way, to avoid irritating or frustrating your people.

Metrics should be developed to provide quantitative feedback on performance toward goals. They should be reviewed monthly, or as often as necessary for the type of work done in your department. Let your staff report their progress, including any problems they may have encountered and their resolution plan. Reporting can be done individually or at departmental meetings.

Inevitably, discussion about personal performance will involve emotional reactions, no matter how hard you try to keep that from happening. If you do not handle feedback and control properly, people will feel threatened. Antagonism and resistance may develop and performance will drop.

Use a control system that builds trust among your employees. Listen to them, understand their concerns and feelings, support them, and engage in mutual problem solving strategies, rather than resort to punishment. When reporting negative variances to higher management, try not to emphasize failure and substandard performance, which can threaten people's careers.

Two-Way Communication

Poor communication between supervisor and employee is one of the biggest problems in the workplace and frequently causes major employee dissatisfaction. Too often managers rely on one-way communication, without even realizing it. They do not ask questions or listen to what others have to say. Listening is a critical skill that many managers lack because they prefer to talk.

Two-way communication happens when both sides get a chance to speak and to listen, and both are open-minded, rather than certain from the start that the other is wrong. Ideally, each person listens to the other without being judgmental or believing that the other person must accept their point of view. If possible, try to let the other person speak first.

Communications aimed at changing someone's mind are rarely effective. If you really listen with an open mind and thereby allow yourself to understand the other person's perspective, you may end up changing your own mind!

Poor communication usually happens because of lack of trust, not because of the way information is communicated. Your people are watching your behavior and will not truly hear you until they trust you. Your staff is watching, and evaluating what you do more than what you say, including how well you listen. Until they like what they see you do, they will care little about what you say.

Seek First to Understand

It's human nature: if you speak first, the other person is unlikely to listen well because he will be too busy running his own argument through his head. This is described in Stephen Covey's book, The 7 Habits of Highly Effective People, in which habit number five is "seek first to understand, then to be understood." This is absolutely true when discussing an issue or a problem, when selling something, and for almost any conversation. Everyone is eager to get their point of view across as soon as possible. So let them.

Let him pour it out while you listen attentively without interruption. After he is done he will be drained and have nothing more to add. At that point there is a good chance he will be able to hear you. And because you listened first you get the extra benefit of knowing what he is thinking, which will help you frame your own response.

At my last job in business development, prospective clients (prospects) came to us to discuss their drug compound and the possibility of having us formulate it into a commercial topical product. Initially, we always made our company presentation first. But sometimes prospects were so anxious to talk about their great technologies that they barely heard what we were saying. Once we realized that, we allowed them to speak first if they wished, which made the more anxious individuals much happier. After their presentation was over, they could relax and listen to what we had to say. And we had the added advantage of tailoring our presentation toward their specific needs because they spoke first, making us more familiar with their projects.

Mutual Trust

One key to getting quality performance from your employees is a trusting relationship. If you do not show your workers that you care about them, they will not care much about what you have to say. Remember, you don't like people because of who they are; you like them because of the way they make you feel.

Establishing that mutual trust between you and your employees will make you a successful manager. If your employees do not trust you, motivation, productivity, job satisfaction, morale, turnover, and departmental pride will all suffer. And your best people will be looking for another job and a better boss.

Trust must be earned. As manager, you must take the time to build credibility and respect. Honesty, integrity, and trust are all linked. If your staff see you as a person of integrity, and you show them respect, you will earn their trust over time. If they question your integrity, they will never trust you. Your actions speak louder than your words, and that is what you will be judged by. As Emerson said: "What you are speaks so loudly that I can't hear what you say." To be credible, you must lead by example.

Everyone wants to be liked, even the best leaders. Never believe a manager who says he does not care if he is liked or not. We work harder and more effectively for people we like, and we like them in direct proportion to how good they make us feel.

To help build mutual trust within your department, show your employees genuine respect by taking the following actions.

- Share as much information as possible.
- Encourage questions and comments — then listen.
- Engage them in goal setting and problem solving.
- Delegate important work, so they can achieve and grow.
- Give them credit for all their work.
- Give them good jobs through job enrichment.
- Let them do their jobs without interfering.
- Recognize and praise them when they do a good job.
- Encourage them continuously.

Process and Workflow Improvement

A task is a unit of work, usually completed by one person, while a process is a group of tasks that together create a result of value to the customer. One task by itself does not create value but, when grouped together to form a whole, they do.

Many company departments are organized based on the functional tasks, and processes often include tasks that cross departmental lines. This mode of operation is not necessarily bad. But when several departments are involved in a process, but nobody has responsibility for the outcome, process improvement is difficult.

Process problems commonly occur because (1) some people are doing tasks that should not be done at all to achieve the desired results, and (2) there is a large time lag in moving the work from one person to another responsible for a different task.

Managers should take the initiative of working with their counterparts in other departments to review and improve the major business processes that cross-departmental lines and provide value to customers. This process may involve eliminating unnecessary tasks; combining, reordering or reassigning tasks; shortening the time lag between tasks; and sharing information.

Within your department, where you have control, you also have processes, and every process, even good ones, can be improved. Since improved productivity is your goal, you should review and optimize departmental workflow and processes on an ongoing basis. After all, doing work as fast, efficiently and effectively as possible is the reason your department exists.

A good way to continuously improve your departmental workflow is to review processes at your monthly department meeting. You cannot review every process, so rotate them. Many routine monthly meetings are of questionable value anyway, so reviewing workflow processes can be an important addition.

Your employees, who are doing the actual work, know more than you do about workflow details and how various tasks interact. Solicit their ideas on how each work process can be improved, how the time between tasks can be shortened, and how costs can be reduced. Perhaps fewer people are truly needed, some steps can be eliminated, tasks can be combined, reordered, or eliminated, or more tasks can be given to fewer people. Every time you review a process, drop the activities that add little value or are redundant. Consolidate, simplify, and speed things up.

In my last position as vice president of a company, we had a process that began when a prospect called to inquire about our services. Initially, I took the call and briefly discussed the client's needs and our services. Then a colleague sent out a confidentiality agreement and another one set up a technical meeting. Yet another person managed the meeting, wrote the proposal and nurtured the prospect until the proposal was signed. So we had a process with multiple steps involving four people in our department. When we discussed process improvement, we decided to consolidate these steps into one job, making the process more efficient and much easier for the prospect, while enriching a job along the way.

Here is a simple way to approach your monthly process improvement discussion:

- Together with your team, analyze the current workflow steps and tasks.
- Discuss issues that need improvement.
- Generate improvement ideas and discuss feelings toward these ideas.
- Decide what changes should be made and how, and move quickly to implement them.

Staff Meetings

When conducted properly and with a clear agenda, staff meetings can be very productive. Otherwise, they are an enormous waste of time. Hold staff meetings only as often as necessary, but not less than once a month.

Think about what you want to achieve at each staff meeting —the critical few things that are most important to the motivation and productivity of your department—and then focus on them. Prepare and circulate an agenda in advance, including topics and time limits, and stick to it. Cut to the chase.

Here are some topics you may want to include in your weekly or monthly staff meeting:

Review Progress Toward Goals

Monthly staff meetings are a good time to review progress towards goals. Ask the head of each section to briefly review metrics toward their goals. If goals are not being met and the problems are significant, hold separate meetings with the people responsible for that particular work. Conclude that meeting by clarifying what follow-up you expect (who will do what, how, and when) and let everyone know when the next review will take place.

Inform and Share Information

Inform your staff about anything important within your department and the company. Unless something is confidential, include as much detail as possible. Share information about company events, performance, sales, profits, market share, productivity, defects, and budgets. Be an open book.

Sharing information helps your people feel valued and enhances their feelings of importance (status) and belonging (social). It reduces any existing feelings of being an outsider looking in, not privy to important information. It shows people you trust them. This is true for everyone in your department, so be sure to include department members at all levels.

Explain to them how the work in your department fits into overall company goals and the products or services being sold. This is important because people want to know they are working for a good company that does meaningful work.

Review Projects

If several people on your team are working on the same project, use your monthly staff meeting as an opportunity to briefly review that particular project. However, if people are working on several projects, do not ask them to discuss details of their work during the meeting. Those not involved will not care and become bored.

Do not waste time going around the room for general project updates. If someone has something important to say, ask that person to add it to the agenda in advance.

Open Discussion

Staff meetings are great opportunities for open discussions about the workplace environment, perceived problems, as well as for sharing company information on activities and events.

Education

Use staff meetings to educate, assuming everyone has a real need for that particular type of technical education or training. Otherwise, do that on an individual basis or at the end of the meeting, so those not interested can leave. Have staff members deliver this education whenever possible.

Process Improvement

Conducting process improvement on an ongoing basis is important, and the monthly staff meeting can be a good opportunity to do this. Pick one process to discuss each month.

Chapter 6 Takeaway

- Write an annual departmental plan that includes goals, which are the backbone of your plan.
- Reaching goals requires commitment, so staff participation in goal setting is mandatory.
- When organizing departmental responsibilities and workflow, focus on the vital few activities that will account for most of your results.
- Staffing is important because without the right people in the right positions all other efforts are futile.
- Use metrics to monitor performance towards goals and to identify problems.
- Evaluate workflow and process improvement to enhance productivity, efficiency and speed.
- Circulate an agenda before every staff meeting and stick to it.
- Build mutual trust through two-way communication, where both parties get to speak openly and both listen to each other.

Decision Making

NOT all decisions are created equal. Some are much more important than others. Some decisions are permanent or difficult to reverse (such as getting married, having kids, building a new factory, starting a new business, or hiring a new person). Others are relatively easy to undo (buying a car or running an ad campaign).

Decision Considerations

Purchase decisions need to consider whether the item incurs only an initial cost or has ongoing annual expenses. For example, when buying a large piece of equipment you have both the initial cost of acquisition and the ongoing costs for insurance, maintenance, and personnel to operate the machine. So before making a decision to buy, rent, or lease an asset, consider all costs and revenue, if any, associated with ownership.

Another important factor to consider is risk. Decisions that could jeopardize the company legally or financially are the ones you must evaluate most strenuously. Finally, there's the "opportunity cost" to consider. Is there something else you could spend your money on instead that may bring greater value to your department?

Most every-day type management decisions you make require a fairly simple cost–benefit analysis. If you have the budget for a purchase and the benefits outweigh the risk, the decision is easy and should help move the department toward its goals.

New Managers: Go Slowly at First

If you are a new manager, take time to get to know your department before you make any major changes or decisions. We have all seen new managers who march in, think they know everything, and make changes quickly, without getting all the facts or feedback. Inevitably, they create resentment and feelings of mistrust. So take your time, ask questions, listen carefully, and build trust. Think about the impact of every decision before you make it. Then make constructive changes slowly when you are sure they are needed.

Team Decisions

As department manager you will be making decisions on a daily basis. For any major decisions, it is important that you include your staff in the process, even if in the end you will make the final decision.

Sometimes it may seem easier to make decisions by yourself. But that is not the only factor to consider. Including your staff is critically important if you want to build mutual trust. Once they can tell you believe in their ability and judgment, they will assume more responsibility later on.

Decisions made with staff input are not always unanimous. You, as department manager, must make the final decision. But the level of staff commitment you get will depend heavily on how you approach the decision and how much you allow others to participate.

After identifying an issue that needs resolution, ask everyone involved for ideas, thoughts and opinions. Use the opportunity to learn about any reservations your people may have and encourage the group to be open to negative reactions and not take them personally. Afterwards, if most staff members are in agreement, make the decision. If not, work on resolving differences (see next section).

Involving your staff will make them feel respected and enhance their self-esteem. They will know they have been heard. Even if they do not agree with your final decision, there is a good chance they will commit to it.

Resolving Differences

Sometimes there will be major differences of opinion among team members on important issues. Strong feelings or significant conflicts are worth working through. If you sweep differences of opinion under the rug to avoid conflict, they will simmer and result in resentment, bad feelings, and a lack of commitment to the final decision. Working through these differences requires open communication.

First, raise the issue and ask for an honest and open discussion from all staff members. Allow them to voice their opinions and back them up. Make it clear that all comments are welcomed, none are bad, and that the staff should listen to what others have to say without interruption. Delve into each opinion until everyone has a clear understanding of all points of view.

An open discussion, without threat to anyone who voices an opinion, is most likely to lead to a better understanding of the issue—sometimes even to staff members changing their opinions and resolving the conflict by consensus.

Other benefits of raising an issue and working through the differences of opinion include:

- The discussion and interplay of ideas may lead to innovation. Individuals present ideas and the team develops them into the best possible solution.
- When the process is successful, all members are committed to implementation of the decision, thereby avoiding resentment as well as possible costs in time or money when commitment to a decision is weak.
- The interplay process strengthens team relationships and builds cooperation and support.

When team members enjoy mutual trust, respect, and support, they will often recognize that many problems are not as serious as they may have seemed at first. They will also be more willing to delegate some decisions to colleagues with the appropriate expertise, because they are trusted. The staff will stick to the more important issues and have less need to show superiority over others. Defensiveness diminishes because there is no need to protect one's ego.

Chapter 7 Takeaway

- Some decisions are much more important than others. Carefully evaluate those that are permanent, difficult to reverse, have high upfront expenditures, large ongoing costs, or that put the company at legal or financial risk.
- Include your staff in major decisions. Doing so leads to commitment on the part of your employees.
- The level of staff commitment you get depends on how you approach the decision-making process and how much you allow others to participate.
- When faced with major differences of opinion, do not try to avoid them. Instead, have an open discussion about the issue.

Hiring Your Employees

HIRING the right people into the right jobs is your most important management duty; otherwise your department will always be mediocre. To succeed, you must hire top-quality people into key positions; conversely, anyone who is not right for a position should be replaced.

Based on my experience, most managers lack focus and skill in this area and do not give high enough priority to proper hiring.

So take the hiring process very seriously. When you hire someone you are adding a spoke to your department wheel, and a weak spoke will drag down the entire department. It makes no sense for you to plan and coordinate departmental work if you do not have the right people in place to get the job done.

Hiring should be a structured process to save time and provide great results. The 80/20 rule applies to employees just as it applies to almost everything, so shoot for job candidates in the top 20 percent in terms of skill and ability when adding a staff member to your team. It may take more time to find that person or cost you more, but it will be well worth it.

You do not get a bargain when you give a job to a weaker candidate for less pay; it will cost you more in the long run. The top 20 percent of workers are superior in knowledge, skill and productivity. It takes less time and money to train them, they get up to speed faster, and you spend less time managing them. They offer you the best chance for success, which means lower turnover costs and fewer headaches.

Do not be penny wise and pound foolish when hiring. Be willing to invest enough money and effort to get the level of talent the position deserves. Set the pay scale high enough to attract the best qualified people. The real bargain is to pay enough to attract a top–20-percent person. This is nothing compared to the time required to train and manage a less capable worker.

Your job is not to be best at the technical or professional work being performed in your department. It is to hire the best people possible. They, not you, will be doing the work. If they are good, you will look very good. The better they are, the more you can sit back, watch productivity grow, and feel great.

Hiring Experienced Candidates

When hiring an experienced candidate, as opposed to one for an entry-level position, your goal should be to find a top-20-percent candidate who has a great attitude, is excited about the job as well as the company, has the right expertise and transferrable skills, has demonstrated major accomplishments in past positions, and comes highly recommended. Also look for candidates with excellent interpersonal and communication skills. Wow! You may not always find the ideal person, but aim as high as you can. Here is a suggested hiring process.

1. Create a List of Top-20-Percent Candidates in Advance

As you become a better manager, turnover in your department will decline, but it will never stop completely. Some people will decide to leave for any number of reasons, such as another job, a promotion, or moving out of the area. To prepare for this, have a list of top-20-percent candidates ready to contact. To build this list, always be on the lookout for qualified people in your industry who have the talent and experience to someday join your team. Chance favors the prepared mind.

Identify top people at conferences, tradeshows, workshops, business meetings, social events, and through your business contacts. You may read that someone in your industry has received an award, a promotion, or a significant new project. Find a way to make contact and to congratulate these people, and, if you see them as possible future candidates, add them to your list.

Once you identify high-potential future candidates for your list, try to develop a personal relationship by contacting them periodically. This takes effort, but you will be happy to have this list when you need it.

Look especially hard for potential candidates inside your own company. These people are pre-screened: their personalities, abilities, communication, and interpersonal skills are already known to you and others within the company. They already know the inner workings of your company, and may even understand the technical or professional aspects of the job you are trying to fill.

In my last company, I hired several excellent employees from other departments, including two from our project management group. We already knew their personalities and capabilities. Their inside experience and knowledge of our specialized topical drug development process was especially valuable. Both of them became very successful in difficult and challenging positions. By comparison, we hired two people from outside the company to do similar work. They both failed and were asked to leave the company. So keep your eyes open for good candidates in other departments, and add them to your candidate list.

2. Update Job Description and Responsibility Table

When a position becomes open, it is time to update both these documents. If this is a new position, create a new job description and responsibility table. These two documents are discussed in depth in Chapter 9. You most likely are familiar with the job description, a document that provides an overview of the position, to whom it reports, its broad responsibilities, and capability requirements. After a position is filled the job description often sits in a file until the next job opening. The responsibility table is a working document that lists each major responsibility, with associated metrics and timelines.

3. Submit the Paperwork for Approval

Before filling an open position, you will be required to complete some documentation, including justification for filling the open position, and cost estimates for recruitment, salary and benefits. For a new position, justification will be even more demanding. Include the job description and responsibility table with the documentation that you send to your supervisor and to HR.

4. Develop Your Hiring Plan with HR

Once you receive authorization to hire, work closely with your HR department to develop a recruitment plan. Devote as much time as necessary to help HR with this process. After all, they are doing this to help you, and if you do not show keen interest in this task, do not expect HR to go out of their way to help. One of the biggest problems in the hiring process is that managers are too busy to devote the necessary time and to react quickly when good candidates are found. I have seen managers sit on applications until the best candidates were gone. This is highly frustrating for the HR department.

You may be lucky and actually find a top-20-percent candidate from your own list of potential candidates. Otherwise, HR can help you find candidates through a wide range of resources, including online recruitment sites, social media, posting ads on websites and in magazines, or through recruiters. Recruiters and search firms can help, but they are expensive and require significant time, energy, and money, and results are often disappointing.

So work with HR to gather information and screen resumes for education, experience, and other qualifications. Then meet with your internal candidates and pre-screen outside candidates by phone.

5. Conduct Phone Screening Interviews

Resumes and online application forms should provide enough information on education, qualifications and work experience for you to determine if a candidate is a reasonable fit for the position. The next step is to schedule telephone-screening interviews with those you like "on paper."

The goal of the telephone interviews is to find top-20-percent candidates who meet your criteria, and to weed out the rest. You obviously want candidates with the appropriate education and experience, success in previous positions, and the qualifications to do the few things absolutely necessary to succeed in this position. But you also want candidates with certain personal skills: enthusiasm, a desire to succeed, and a keen interest in the position they applied for. Personal attributes (soft skills) can be assessed more fully when a candidate is invited in for face-to-face interviews.

Preparation for Interview

Before you conduct the phone screening interviews, send a confidential copy of the job description to each candidate so they can fully understand the primary responsibilities and the qualifications required for this job. Also, depending on the type of job being filled, ask for samples of their work or give them a small assignment to help assess their skills.

Candidate resumes should show colleges attended and degrees earned, work experience (with exact dates) and major responsibilities and accomplishments in each prior position. If some of this information is missing from the resume, ask the candidate to provide it in advance. You will need it to help guide the interview.

The phone screening Interview

Introduce yourself, the company and briefly describe the position. Make sure you control the interview and not allow the candidate to take over and make you do the talking. Using the resume as a guide, ask each question and then listen carefully and take notes. Pay attention to the facts, but also try to get a feeling about a candidate's attitude, level of enthusiasm, communication skills, and thought process.

Determine the candidate's level of interest in this position, and the reason for it. Since they have a copy of the job description, candidates should have a good idea of the job scope, duties and responsibilities. Hopefully they have done some research and have questions about the company and the job. If not, that is a big red flag.

A technique known as "behavioral interviewing" focuses on asking candidates questions about similar work done in the past, level of success, achievements, and how problems were handled. Assessing past behavior is important because people tend to behave the same way in the future.

Suggested telephone Interview questions

Assess Job Interest (20 minutes)

- Why do you want this job? (Probe until satisfied.)
- Why are you a good fit for this position? (Probe.)
- What experience has prepared you for this job? (Probe.)
- Why should I hire you?
- What questions do you have about this position?
- What questions do you have about our company?

Continue the interview only if the candidate has impressed you so far. If you feel the person is not a good fit, thank him and terminate the interview. Explain that at this stage in the process you are screening several candidates. Then follow up with a classy rejection letter.

Job History (20-30 minutes)

Confirm companies and dates. For each relevant position ask:

- What were your primary responsibilities? (Listen and take notes.)
- What were your major accomplishments? (Listen and take notes.)
- What did you like most about this position?
- What did you like least about this position?
- Why did you leave this position?

Education (10 minutes)

Confirm schools, degrees earned and specific dates for recent graduates. Question any significant time gaps.

For fairly recent graduates ask:

- What classes did you take that will help in this position?
- What grades did you get in these classes?
- Tell me about any special achievements in college.

After the interview, review your notes and consider the responses. Did you see any behavior patterns? Was there a history of accomplishments and success? Are past experiences and major responsibilities good training for this job? Can the candidate do the few things absolutely necessary to succeed in this position?

Also consider how excited the candidate is about the company and this position, and the reasons why. Did she project a high level of energy and drive to get things done? After this evaluation determine if this is a top-20-percent candidate who compares favorably with other top candidates, and should be invited in for a face-to-face interview.

6. Conduct Face-To-Face Interviews

Invite final candidates inside for face-to-face interviews. The goal is to confirm what you suspected after each telephone interview: that the candidate has the right qualifications and technical experience, and can do the few things absolutely necessary to succeed in this position.

Equally important, face-to-face interviews will help you determine if a candidate has the personality and soft skills necessary to fit into the job, department and company. You want excellent interpersonal and communication skills, creative problem solving skills, drive, enthusiasm, and the determination to get things done.

Suggested interviews

HR may try to schedule a long list of interviews with a variety of candidates because that is the traditional way to do it. But if possible, do not waste time having candidates interview with several co-workers who do not really care and most likely are terrible interviewers. Here are the interviews you should consider scheduling.

- One interview with a representative from HR
- One or two interviews with your top subject matter people to confirm the candidate's technical or professional knowledge, expertise and achievements
- One interview with a colleague from inside or outside the department who will work most closely with this position (optional)
- Lunch with several department members to help assess soft skills
- A 1.5-2 -hour interview with the hiring manager, to assess interpersonal and communication skills, problem solving ability, energy level, drive to achieve, friendliness, and demeanor.
- An interview with your supervisor, if required (optional)

Assign interviewer responsibilities

Most people are not trained to interview and do a poor job of it. They are likely to spend more time talking about themselves than questioning and listening to the candidate. Candidates love this because they do not have to talk much. In the end, the interviewer learns little about the candidates but likes them because they listen so well. This is why you want to keep the number of interviewers to a minimum.

Give each interviewer the candidate's resume, the job description, and a list of specific areas to cover during the interview. Ask for a report after each interview. When interviewers have a goal they are more likely to stay on target. Ask the interviewers to do the following:

- Review the job description and resume in advance.

- Break the ice and introduce themselves and their area of responsibility.
- Control the interview and not allow the candidate to take the upper hand.

Technical interviews

Ask your technical interviewers to focus on the candidates' subject-matter knowledge and achievements to help determine if the candidate is technically qualified for the position. Discuss prior jobs in which the candidate did similar work. Ask specific technical questions. Probe for achievements. And ask about problems encountered and how they were solved.

Have them present a subject-matter problem to the candidate and listen carefully to how he would solve it. This will help them understand the candidate's level of technical or professional competence, how he or she thinks, and the person's problem solving skills. Ask each interviewer to write a brief assessment report after the interview.

Lunch interview

Interpersonal and social skills are as important as technical and professional skills. Have a few staff members take the candidate to lunch, ask numerous personal questions and see how the candidate interacts and behaves in a social setting.

Have your team observe "the waiter rule." You can learn a lot about a person's character by the way he treats the waiter, or the receptionist, your assistant, or others he makes contact with. Avoid people who have a situational value system, who turn the charm on and off depending on the status of the person they are interacting with.

Hiring manager's interview

An hour and a half to two hours may seem like a long time to spend with a candidate, but keep in mind that hiring the right person is one of the most important things you will do as a manager. The decision is not easily reversible, and if you make a mistake you will spend far more time trying to fix it. The long interview is especially important if you plan to make an offer after only one round of interviews. However, if your company policy is to bring the finalists back for a second interview, then a long initial interview becomes less important.

Your primary goal is to get to know the candidate as well as possible on a personal level, to evaluate communication skills, problem solving ability, energy level, drive to achieve, friendliness, and demeanor. In the end, you must decide if the candidate is a good fit for the position and is someone you will enjoy working with on a daily basis. Try to spend enough time with the candidate to uncover his or her real personality.

During the first round of interviews try to be the last interviewer of the day, and get feedback from the others before you start your questioning. If they have a strong negative impression of the candidate for solid reasons, you can plan for a short interview.

Use the candidate's resume and work history form to help guide your questions. Since you have more time than you did in the telephone interview, you can use a behavioral interviewing technique by asking open-ended questions, probing, and listening carefully.

Start with the question: "Tell me about yourself." This allows the candidate to decide what's important, and hopefully to talk about his or her experiences and accomplishments. This helps you determine if a candidate is a logical thinker and an effective communicator.

If at all possible, and especially when filling high-level positions, the hiring manager should try to have breakfast (or dinner) with serious candidates. If you take the candidate to breakfast, keep the conversation light. Ask him to tell you about himself (hobbies, interests) so you can have a good two-way discussion. Answer any questions the candidate may have. Mainly, observe the candidate's demeanor and behavior.

Suggested face-to-face Interview questions for hiring manager

Opening Questions

- Tell me about yourself.
- Why are you interested in this position?
- Why are you qualified for this position?
- What do you want in your next job?
- What do you want in your next supervisor?
- What are your career goals?

Education

Ask about the candidate's educational experience provided he or she graduated less than ten years ago.

- Tell me about your college experience.
- How well did you do in school?
- What classes did you take that will help in this position?
- Did you have any special achievements in college?
- Did you work while in college?

Job History

For each relevant position, confirm job title, start and end dates. Question any time gap in work history.

- Tell me about this job.
- What were your primary responsibilities? (Listen and probe.)
- What were your major achievements? (Listen and probe.)
- What was the secret to your success in this job?
- Tell me about the team you worked with?
- Tell me about a problem you encountered and how you solved it.
- How did you set priorities? Give me an example.
- What did you like most about this job?
- What did you like least about this job?
- Why did you leave this job?

Closing Questions

- What is the worst company culture you have worked in, and why?
- How did you deal with that bad environment?
- What was the best company culture you have worked in, and why?
- What would your coworkers say are your strengths?
- What would they say are your weaknesses?
- Where do you need improvement or more experience?
- Tell me about a job that wasn't what you expected and how you dealt with it.
- Do you prefer to work alone or with a team, and why?

- Tell me about working on a team that failed.
- What was your role and how did you handle the failure?

What to look for

Obviously, you want someone with the required technical or professional skills to do the actual work. Interviews conducted by your staff will help determine this.

Look for people who are enthusiastic with good interpersonal skills, who like doing this kind of work and are excited about this job. Weed out the people who have the right credentials with the wrong personality. Piece together the candidate's work history and look for performance patterns to help predict future performance. Look for behavioral trends, evidence of achievement and ability, ambition, intelligence, enthusiasm, and a good work ethic.

Also look for attributes that could be problematic. You want someone you would enjoy working with on a daily basis. In some cases you can teach people new skills, but it is very difficult to teach people to be kind-hearted, compassionate and nice.

Hiring someone with success doing similar work will shorten the learning curve, so make sure to consider qualified people within your company, since they already know the ropes.

7. Collect Feedback After the Interviews

Ask for feedback as quickly as possible from all individuals who interviewed the candidate. Do it the same day while it is still fresh in their minds. If possible, convene a short meeting, or else go see each person to discuss the candidate. Then, compare and rank all the final candidates. Hopefully you will have found someone you feel great about and can move forward on.

8. Check References

The goal of reference checks is to confirm your decision to make an offer to a specific candidate. Talking with people who have worked with the candidate will help to validate that person's strengths, weaknesses and potential. Check several references unless you know the candidate personally.

Routine reference checks are a bit of a farce because candidates only provide names of people who will say good things. References usually give glowing endorsements or decline to talk by saying their company policy is not to comment. Some people will not talk because they are afraid of potential litigation.

A better way of checking references is for you to decide what former supervisors and colleagues you wish to speak with, and obtain the candidate's permission to speak to those people. Ask the candidate to help schedule evening or weekend telephone calls, but not while the reference is at work. Do reference checks by phone so there is nothing in writing, unless a reference wishes to send you a positive letter or e-mail. Listen for what is said and especially for what is not said.

Keep reference calls short and professional. Here are some suggested questions:

- In what situation did you work with this person?
- What do you think are his strengths? Any examples?
- What qualities was he known for?
- In what areas did he struggle?

- How would you describe his energy level?
- How would you describe his ability to prioritize?
- How good was he at getting things done?
- Please talk about his interactions with coworkers?
- How did you feel about his overall job performance?
- Would you hire him again?

9. Make the Offer

Once you find the right person for the job and you are happy with your reference checks, make the offer as soon as possible. Keep in mind that your competitors can also recognize top talent.

Sometimes managers are pressured into hiring fast, so they drop the quality bar. Do not fall into this trap. It is better to spend the extra time upfront. The decision to hire someone is not easily reversible; not hiring the wrong person is as important as hiring the right one. A bad hire will cost you time and money, so do not hire until you find the right person; but once you do, act fast.

Hiring New College Graduates

When hiring new college graduates just entering the workforce, who have little or no relevant work experience, you are looking primarily for ambitious, high energy people with good interpersonal skills and a sincere interest in the position and your company. You want people who are good listeners, team players, fast learners, able to take responsibility and solve problems, and who do not blame others for their failures.

Working continuously from a young age is an indicator of a strong work ethic. Participation in sports indicates competitiveness, the desire to win, and the skills needed to be a team player. Coming from an entrepreneurial family is good. Educational success and participation in activities like sports, band, or clubs gives you an idea about a person's level of ambition.

Here is a suggested process for hiring recent college graduates into entry-level positions.

1. Screen Resumes

The resume and application form should provide enough personal, educational, and work experience information for you to determine if a candidate is at least qualified for an entry-level position. Set up a telephone screening interviews with the best candidates "on paper."

2. Conduct Telephone Screening Interviews

The goal of the telephone interviews is to find candidates who meet most of the criteria mentioned above and to weed out the rest. Since these candidates have little experience, you will be looking primarily for enthusiasm, ambition, a desire to succeed, academic success, and a keen interest in the position they applied for. Personal attributes (soft skills) can be better assessed when a candidate is invited for face-to-face interviews.

Suggested telephone interview questions

Assess Job Interest (10 minutes)

- What are you looking for in a job?

- Why do you want this particular job? (Probe until satisfied.)
- Why are you a good fit for this job?
- What questions do you have about this position?
- What questions do you have about our company?

Education (20 minutes)

Look for degrees and specific dates. Question any significant time gaps.

- In college, what were your grades and where did you graduate in your class?
- What classes did you take that will help you with this job?
- What extracurricular activities did you pursue in college?
- What jobs did you hold while in college?
- Did you have any special achievements while in college?

Job History (10 minutes)

New college graduates will have little relevant work experience. For each relevant position, ask:

- Tell me about your responsibilities in this job.
- What were your major accomplishments?
- What did you like most about this job?
- What did you like least about this job?

If the candidate has impressed you with the right education, skills to succeed in this position, energy and personality, then discuss next steps. Otherwise thank the person for talking with you and follow-up with a nice rejection letter.

After the interview, review your notes. Does the candidate have the education and technical skills needed in this entry-level position? Can she learn the things necessary to succeed? Is she enthusiastic with a history of accomplishments and extracurricular activities in college? Is she excited about this position and your company and does she compare favorably to other top candidates? Then determine if the candidate should be invited in for face-to-face interviews along with the other finalists.

3. Conduct Face-to-Face Interviews

Face-to-face interviews with each entry-level candidate will help you reinforce the impression made over the phone, plus help you better assess the individual's interpersonal and communication skills. Before the interview, ask for a work sample or give a small assignment to assess an individual's skills more directly.

Spend at least an hour with the candidate. Ask the HR department and one or two other staff members to meet with the candidate. Have a group of people in the department take him or her to lunch and ask several questions to help assess interpersonal and social skills.

Suggested Face-to-face Interview Questions For New Graduates

Opening Questions (20-30 minutes)

- Tell me about yourself and your family.
- What are you looking for in a job?
- Why are you interested in this position?
- What questions do you have about this position?

- Why are you qualified for this position?
- What are you especially good at?
- What are you not so good at?
- What are you looking for in your next supervisor?
- What would your friends say are your strengths?
- What would your friends say are your weaknesses?
- What are your career goals?
- What questions do you have about our company?

Education (20 minutes)

Discuss their education experience, degrees and specific dates. Question any significant time gaps.

- Tell me about your grades.
- Where did you graduate in your class?
- Tell me about any classes that would help you in this job.
- What extracurricular activities did you pursue in college?
- What jobs did you hold while in college?
- Did you have any special achievements while in college?

Job History (10 minutes)

New college graduates will have little relevant work experience. For each relevant position:

- Tell me about your responsibilities in this job.
- What were your major accomplishments?
- What did you like most about this job?
- What did you like least about this job

4. Check References and Make the Offer

While references are less valuable for entry-level employees, you should still check a few, such as a college professor or former supervisor in a relevant job. Keep the calls short and professional.

Suggested questions:

- How do you know this person?
- What do you think are his or her strengths? Any examples?
- What about weaknesses? Any examples?
- How would you describe the person's energy level?
- What qualities was he or she known for?
- How well did he or she get along with others?
- Would you hire this person if it was your decision?

When you are confident you found the right person for the job, make the offer.

Early Education and Orientation

It takes a little time and effort to plan an orientation program in advance, but when people start a new job they have apprehension. They need to feel that they belong and that they are working for a good company that does meaningful work and treats people right. It is up to you to make them feel welcomed.

Write out a plan for each new employee, starting with the first day on the job. Welcome them to the company as soon as they arrive. After they go to HR for benefits orientation and paperwork, meet with them to answer their questions and to explain their orientation schedule for the first week.

An upfront orientation during the first week of work will give each employee a great initial impression of the company and a feeling of belonging. This helps build loyalty and commitment. As manager, you only have one chance to make a great first impression.

As soon as you can, introduce them to colleagues they will interact with inside and outside the department. Schedule meetings with the people they will interact with most. Give them a visual overview of the company, products and services. If you do not have an overview, develop one. Give them a copy of the organizational chart so they can see exactly where they fit in.

Within the first month educate them about your company, products and services. In addition to informing them, you will reinforce the feeling of belonging and of being part of a good organization. People want a sense of purpose and wish to contribute to something worthwhile. Tell them about your company's core purpose and how their particular job fits into the whole. Remind them they are working for a great company that only hires the best people.

Chapter 8 Takeaway

- Devote much time to the process of hiring the right people into the right jobs. It is your most important management responsibility.
- Working with HR, use a structured process to save time and get great results.
- Create a list of top internal and external candidates to use first when you need to hire someone.
- Provide rapid education and orientation for new employees within the first weeks on the job.
- Help them understand the company and where their job fits in.

CHAPTER 9

Individual Management

CHAPTER 6 covered topics that relate to management of the overall department. This chapter will discuss topics that relate to managing the individual employee.

Job Descriptions

Your HR group should require a job description for every position in your department and provide guidelines and the desired format. If not, you should write a job description for each position *anyway*. At the very least, this document should include job responsibilities, desired qualifications (education, technical skills, experience), to whom the position reports within the department, as well as desired personal attributes, such as interpersonal and communication skills.

If you go beyond the minimum job description requirements and put extra time and thought into it, this document will be much more useful when recruiting and hiring, as well as at annual employee performance review time.

Carefully consider the unique qualifications required for each job. How technical is the position and what level of education and knowledge is really needed? Must the new employee have the skills to be able to hit the road running or can the person be trained on the job? Consider if the necessary skills are transferable from one industry to another. For example, analytical testing may be similar across industries, but marketing techniques may differ significantly across industries and this may significantly slow down someone attempting to move from one industry to another

At my last company, we twice hired inexperienced but well-educated technical people to write product development proposals. Both failed because they could not master the details of our drug development process. On the other hand, a chemist hired in the analytical department, who had experience outside the pharmaceutical industry, turned out to be a very productive worker and eventually became that department's manager.

Under responsibilities, add some measurable metrics you expect from an ideal candidate and describe what a top performance would look like when a responsibility is satisfactorily met. Include three to five things that a candidate absolutely must be able to do to succeed in this position.

This enhanced job description will help everyone, including the candidates for the position, to clearly understand what is expected of them. It is also valuable as a recruiting tool.

When creating a job description, remember that people need important, meaningful work, and must be able to utilize their skills. So make each job as challenging and as complete (enriched) as possible.

For all their value, job descriptions are not very useful as daily working documents. That is where the responsibility table comes in.

Responsibility Tables

Studies show that a wide discrepancy often exists between how the employee and the manager perceive the employee's role and performance expectations. To avoid such misunderstandings, make sure that you and each of your employees are in clear agreement about responsibilities and expectations from the very beginning.

The two-column responsibility table I created serves as a working tool throughout the year, and is updated as needed. It is much more useful than the job description, especially since that is not always readily available.

The responsibility table is unique to each job and should be developed jointly by the manager and the employee.

In column 1, list each of the employee's major responsibilities, as you both understand them. For this task use the job description as a guide, as well as department goals, and common sense. In column 2, add quantitative metrics and timelines to show what constitutes success for each responsibility. Create a way to measure the performance you want. Use metrics to define what top-level performance would look like for each major responsibility.

For a salesperson, metrics may include number of sales calls, number of new accounts, or revenue levels to be achieved in a certain time period. For a writer it might be the quality and number of articles written per month.

Here are some areas where the responsibility table will be useful:

- Conducting annual performance reviews
- Monthly goal monitoring
- Organizing department workflow
- Balancing individual workloads
- Assigning work to those who like doing it
- Enriching jobs

Individual Goal Setting

The perception of movement towards a goal helps build feelings of achievement and self-esteem. Just as your department need goals, so do individual employees.

Individual goals are usually set annually, right after corporate goals are issued and department goals are set. Make sure to monitor and review individual goals at least quarterly to determine progress and to modify them if necessary.

Using the responsibility table, work with the employee to set specific, measurable, challenging but achievable goals that are consistent with and support departmental goals. Be sure to include some personal development goals for each employee.

Never set employee goals alone or you will create resentment and a lack of commitment. By working on goals together you are building mutual trust and the employee is more likely to commit to accomplishing the goals.

Also make sure the goals that are very clear and free of ambiguities. The clearer the endpoints and ways to achieve them, the less chance for future misunderstanding or procrastination on the part of the employee.

Training

New employees joining your department will need training to do their job effectively in a new environment. Even if they had similar experience elsewhere, they will need some instruction and direction to fully understand how their job fits in your department. Ask new hires frequently about how they are doing and if they need anything, including more training.

If you have senior people who are good at working with new people, consider a mentor/protégé relationship for the new employees. Just make sure to talk to the potential mentor first to get their consent. To be a mentor may seem like an honor, but not everyone feels comfortable in this task or can spare the time.

Training is not a perk reserved exclusively for new employees. Existing staff members may lack the job training they need to succeed, especially in a rapidly changing field. If an employee seems to lack motivation or is underperforming, training may solve the problem. After any training is completed, test the workers to make sure the investment has achieved its objectives.

Training is one of the most powerful tools and motivators you have at your disposal for current employees who are not adequately trained for their jobs, as well as for new employees who are anxious to learn, grow and contribute in their new positions.

Coaching

Once you have the right people in the right positions, the jobs are enriched, responsibilities are clear, the training is done, and the goals are set, you are ready to move into the coaching mode.

In fact, much of your day-to-day time should be spent on coaching—the art of improving the performance of your employees. Coaching is used to build up their skills, oversee their progress, help them solve their problems, overcome conflicts, brainstorm, develop career paths, and prepare them for promotion.

Think about it. A coach does not play the game; he develops his players to be the best they can be at playing it. A manager does the same thing—develops his staff to be at its best, on the job and in achieving their goals. After all, as manager you are judged on the results of the work your people do.

Coaching employees, however, is not exactly like coaching a sports team. Sports are far less democratic. When a sports coach is doing his job, the coaching usually consists of a one-way conversation. The coach talks and the player listens. There is some give and take, but not much. As a business coach, you need to listen much more and ask your employees to suggest alternative solutions to problems. Then, when appropriate, you should present additional, alternative solutions based on your broader range of experience.

As manager, most likely you are one of the most experienced people in the department. The best way to use this knowledge is by coaching your people when they need help.

Coaching is also very important when delegating responsibilities. When you delegate a project, you must make sure the employee clearly understands the assignment, the expectations and the timeline. That is where the coaching comes in. As the confidence and competence of your staff improves as a result of it, so will their self-esteem and their willingness to take on additional responsibility.

Here are some situations where coaching can be very effective.

- *Skill building:* Train and educate new employees on how to break larger assignments into smaller tasks and guide them through each task, as needed.
- *Goal setting:* Help set individual work and career development goals.
- *Work progress:* Help employees work through any difficulties encountered during a special assignment or in their regular responsibilities.
- *Problem solving:* Review employee problems and their causes, and brainstorm together to find solutions.
- *Personal conflicts:* Help diffuse disagreements between employees.

Coaching will only work when mutual trust is established. The employee must feel safe enough to speak openly and honestly, and the manager must be willing to listen carefully with an open mind. Let the employee speak first and listen without interrupting. Draw out, discuss and clarify thoughts and ideas to help the employee decide how to complete a project or solve a problem. Be supportive, a careful listener, and an active catalyst.

Because of their limited experience, newer and younger employees will be aware of fewer solutions when approaching a problem. As a coach and manager with more experience, you will be in a position to help them brainstorm and come up with alternate solutions. Just one more alternative may be what is needed to solve a problem. Spend enough time with your newer employees to make sure you have addressed all their questions and concerns.

Be careful not to dictate a solution. That is not coaching (except in sports). When workers come to you for help, do not tell them what to do. Instead, help them understand the various alternatives and how to choose the best action to solve the problem. Encourage your people to consider several alternatives and then reach their own conclusion.

The Coaching Process

- Define the problem to solve.
- Analyze the situation and the causes with the employee.
- Let the employee present alternate solutions.
- Build on these ideas and suggest additional alternatives.
- Help the worker select the best actions to pursue.
- Agree on specific actions to take and the timing to solve the problem.
- Review progress at the next session.

Your staff wants to have positive time with you, so be sure to schedule individual weekly or monthly meetings to discuss progress on major projects, answer any questions, and to help solve any problems they may have. Just the act of interacting with your employees will help build their confidence and self-esteem, feelings of belonging and mutual respect.

Public Speaking

The ability of your people to speak in public is critical to their development and advancement, especially those at higher levels in the organization. Ask them to contribute at meetings and to give presentations whenever they can. However, be aware that speaking to a group can be very difficult for some people. I know, because I suffered from panic attacks for several years, including during a period of time when I interviewed and was hired for the position of vice president at a major corporation.

These attacks continued during meetings and presentations. After studying the problem I learned that it is the anticipation of an attack that often makes it happen. Once I understood what panic attacks are, I was better able to work through them, and eventually they subsided.

While most people's fear of public speaking is not as extreme and does not cause panic attacks, it is very important for you to understand that many of your employees are most likely afraid of public speaking. Do not force them to speak, but privately encourage them to attend Toastmasters or a similar organization to gain confidence speaking in front of a crowd and to overcome their fears. Emphasize that to grow a career, one must be able to contribute at meetings, give speeches, and make presentations in front of sizable groups.

Friendship

Can a supervisor be a friend to his direct reports? Some people say no because the employees will try to take advantage of your friendship. Not true. The idea that a manager cannot be friendly with his staff is a throwback to the old autocratic, Theory X style of management.

When people work together in a professional environment defined by honesty, respect and trust, a degree of friendship usually develops.

Friendship and mutual respect enables two-way communication and opens up discussions on topics that cannot be raised without trust. Most likely, the employee will work even harder for you if you show interest in them as individuals, not just employees. Occasionally this can backfire, and an employee will try to take advantage of your friendship, so be sure to remain in control by monitoring to make sure the work is done and goals are met.

Employee Problem Solving

Significant employee problems should be addressed with vigor before the problem gets out of hand and impacts others in your department. Problems can involve either performance (affecting an employee's work) or behavior in the workplace (e.g., tardiness or conflict with a coworker). Either way, you must either strengthen the weak link or eliminate it.

Performance Problems

Poor performance can result from any number of reasons, including a poor employee-supervisor relationship, a bad job, inadequate training, a problem in the workplace environment, or a personal issue at work or at home. Instead of trying to guess and judge, sit down with the employee to discuss the problem openly, understand its root cause, and jointly seek a solution.

1. Lack of direction and feedback

About half of performance problems result from poor communications, particularly a lack of proper direction or feedback from the supervisor. The employee does not know what to do, when to do it, or what the final product should look like. To address the problem, discuss the issue openly and set clear, specific goals. Make use of the employee's responsibility table to provide proper direction to the employee. Discuss the issue in depth, answer questions, and clear up any misunderstandings. For new employees, review their work frequently to make sure they are on target.

Frequent feedback is important for employees to know how well they are performing. If they do a good job, give positive feedback. If not, develop an improvement plan together as soon as you are aware of a problem.

2. Lack of training

Even when the employee knows what to do, he or she may sometimes lack the knowledge or skill to perform the entire job well. With the rapid advances in technology, for example, keeping up to speed with expectations may be difficult without additional training.

Because of pride, however, an employee may not admit he lacks training or a critical skill. So first ascertain that the person knows exactly what is expected of him. Then determine what type of training, if any, is needed, and provide it.

3. A bad job

Typically, if you notice poor performance (e.g., frequent mistakes or missed deadlines) from an employee who understands his or her job responsibilities and is adequately trained, you are likely to assume the problem is a bad attitude or poor motivation. But the real reason may be the job itself, if it offers little responsibility or few opportunities to achieve something meaningful.

Attempts to improve performance by trying to improve someone's attitude will not work if the job is bad. That is because attitude does not cause behavior. It is the other way around. An employee's attitude is derived from the job you are asking the person to do.

Employees cannot be motivated to do a good job if there is no good job to do. Conversely, if a worker is happy with his job, most likely his attitude will reflect that.

So when you see a performance problem from an employee who has adequate direction and training, instead of asking, "what is wrong with him?" ask yourself "is there anything about his job that could be impeding performance?" He may have a job where he repeatedly encounters some silly rule or cumbersome process, or the job may be boring, fragmented, or offer little autonomy.

If you determine that poor performance is indeed the result of a bad job, you need to take immediate steps to enrich that job. Once you do, performance is likely to improve.

Sometimes, if a worker has a responsibility she just does not like to do, it is best to find someone else who does not mind doing it. Focus on getting the job done by playing into each person's strengths.

Behavioral Problems

While unrelated to the job itself, behavioral problems—such as tardiness, taking excess sick time, or confrontations with other employees—occur in the workplace and need to be addressed quickly. The reasons for these problems can range from personal difficulties to a bad job. It is up to you to identify the cause.

Just like with performance problems, do not make a snap judgment. Instead, sit down with the employee and discuss the problem, the cause, and seek a solution together. Consider that the person may be going through a real-life emergency. You will not know until you ask.

Explain to the employee that you understand that something serious must be causing the problem. Tell him you are sorry you have not established a relationship that would allow him to take you in his confidence and give you a chance to help. Consider this person a valuable employee with a problem that can be solved, unless you decide your efforts are futile and you are better off finding and training a replacement.

Focus on the behavior, not the attitude

While you may think a person's behavior is bad, he or she may disagree and think the actions were perfectly logical given the circumstances and available alternatives. So start by trying to understand the options the person had and why he or she chose one that you did not like.

Since none of us can read another person's mind, it is best to focus on the behavior we actually see and not on attitudes we perceive. Make an effort to separate the person from the negative behavior. Say something like, "I like you very much, but I'm concerned that you've been late a lot lately. Can we talk about it?"

Behavior can be changed regardless of attitude; once the behavior has been improved the attitude usually follows. Positive behavior followed by positive consequences will become a self-fulfilling prophecy.

If the behavioral problem is major, make sure to document it. If the problem persists and cannot be solved, even after you have exhausted correction attempts, work with HR to terminate this person within all legal requirements.

Chapter 9 Takeaway

- Write a job description for everyone in your department.
- Work with each employee to develop his or her responsibility table.
- Work with each employee to develop personal goals consistent with departmental goals.
- Use senior people in your department as mentors for new hires whenever possible.
- Make sure all your employees have proper training to do their jobs.
- Spend significant time coaching employees. Listen carefully and offer alternatives, but let them decide how to proceed as long as their ideas are reasonable.
- Encourage your staff to make presentations and develop public speaking skills, which are critical for their career development.
- Most employees work harder if the supervisor is a friend, so try to build a good relationship with your employees, but always monitor performance toward goals.
- When you see performance problems, look first for poor direction and feedback, lack of adequate training, or a bad job.
- Use a collaborative approach to openly discuss the cause of behavioral problems and to agree on a solution.

Performance Reviews

A s you read this chapter, keep in mind that people can never totally separate their rational self from the emotional one. It does not matter if the issue is a performance review or a general discussion: the more serious the issue, the greater the emotional factor.

Handling Emotions

Attempts to set aside emotions through conscious effort or verbal persuasion will fail because most of our emotional response comes from our subconscious mind. Since we cannot eliminate our emotions, the best we can do is to prepare ourselves to keep them at bay and not allow ourselves to react emotionally or blow up.

If you must deliver bad news or discuss a personal problem with an employee, try to prepare the recipient in advance to reduce the emotional impact.

In my last job, when I was told something that upset me, I was prone to moving rapidly from a 1 to a 10 on a ten-point emotional scale. It became a bit of an inside joke: before delivering bad news, my staff would first ask me where I was on the scale. That tipped me off that bad news was coming, which helped me control my negative reaction. This approach works to some degree, so when you are delivering bad news, allow some time for mental preparation.

The Annual Performance Review

The typical annual performance review is required by most companies and dreaded by most employees. As a throwback to the old Theory X, command-and-control style of management, it is often a one-sided meeting where the supervisors tells employees about their strengths and weaknesses, what they did right or wrong over the past year, and where they need to improve. Meanwhile employees sit and listen, burning up inside.

Negative comments during performance reviews will undoubtedly ignite strong emotions and put employees on the defensive, which in turn will cloud their thinking and cause them to ignore or misinterpret the facts.

A criticism based on the supervisor's subjective perceptions cannot be objective. Nor can a monologue where the boss points out the employee's deficiencies ever be a productive exchange of ideas. Suggestions for improvement are not likely to be heard or retained. It is little wonder that most annual performance reviews are so dreaded.

Problems with the Annual Review

In his 2010 book entitled *Get Rid Of The Performance Review!*, Samuel Culbert, a professor at the University of California, Los Angeles, calls the annual performance review one of the most damaging of all corporate activities. He questions how anything so destructive and universally despised can continue to plague the workplace. Culbert believes executives are blind to the damage created by these reviews. If only they could understand that a trusting relationship with their people is the best tool in obtaining high-quality work, they would never allow the traditional one-sided, supervisor-dominated performance reviews to continue.

Below are some other major concerns regarding the annual performance review as it is done most of the time.

The link to pay

Since reviews and pay raises tend to occur annually, they become linked. Employees try to put a positive spin on their contributions so they can receive the maximum possible raise. Similarly, they will not admit to the need for further training. The supervisor, on the other hand, wants to discuss performance improvements, skill limitations, and development needs. The employees bite their tongues because they fear that the anything could be held against them, and that the supervisor's opinion will determine everything from pay increases to work assignments and career progress.

I once rated a well-deserving employee "excellent" on a few attributes. But my supervisor, the CEO, told me to bring these high ratings back to mid-range. He was afraid employees would expect larger raises if we rated them too high. Talk about demotivating! I was so angry that I asked my supervisor if he had ever read a book on motivation. I do not suggest you do the same unless you plan to retire. I later apologized.

The point is, some people play games with performance reviews, and that is another reason why most people hate them.

Suggested changes do not occur

In the common scenario of the supervisor finding fault and the employee being afraid to speak out, no two-way communication can take place, in which case even the most valid feedback will most likely be ignored. Research shows that supervisors' requests for changes in behavior during performance reviews do not usually happen. One study showed that in only ten percent of cases both the worker and the supervisor remembered the request and also agreed that the change had occurred. Employees do not seem to hear or retain negative comments delivered during performance reviews.

Ratings differ by manager

To make matters worse, performance review ratings will vary depending on who is doing the review. Assessments of how well employees are doing are clearly subjective measurements. Different managers will rate the same employee differently.

One study evaluated 6,000 employees each of whom were rated by multiple supervisors on various attributes using a seven-point scale. The results showed that these assessments could vary by as much as 62 percent for the same employee, even when someone was rated as outstanding by one of the supervisors.

Every manager approaches the review process with his or her own prejudices and agendas. Assessment of an employee is invariably dependent on these biases. Considering that, how much value do these ratings really have when it comes to allotting pay raises? Not much. This process is so subjective that it may do more harm than good.

I worked at a pharmaceutical company where the medical unit director rated all of his people 5 (excellent) because, as he put it, "I only hire excellent people." While his people loved his rating system, the company did not. To the extent to which performance reviews were linked to pay, his people most likely were getting higher raises than their equally-qualified peers in other departments. Such inequality is bound to lead to resentment and frustration in the workplace.

Effective Annual Performance Reviews

Like it or not, the annual performance review is an institution that will not vanish anytime soon. And if it is required by your company, you must do it. But you can exercise some control over how to make these reviews as successful as possible and not demotivate your people. Here are some tips on how you can make the review constructive and positive.

To help employees prepare for it, give them a copy of the entire review form, including the attribute-rating sheet, and ask them to complete it in advance. Also ask them to review their responsibility table, prepare a list of their major accomplishments during the past year, including how well their goals were met, and to think about their development needs for next year.

The annual review should not result in any big surprises, provided you meet with each employee at least monthly to review work projects and goals. If there are areas where an employee must improve, tell them as soon as this becomes apparent. Do not wait until the annual performance review to raise negative issues and demoralize the employee.

When conducting the annual review, try to create an environment where the worker feels safe enough to have an open and honest dialog. Try to build trust, give encouragement, tell them what you think they are doing well, correct a few minor problems if needed, and leave the employee feeling motivated.

With good employees this process is easy. But the general principle is the same even with employees who do not perform as well.

Try to criticize as little as possible. Instead, use the review as a once-a-year opportunity to officially discuss positive accomplishments and show employees how you can help them do even better. This way you help build their confidence and self-esteem. With an atmosphere of trust and straight talk, some people might even dare to suggest areas where they think they need to improve.

Focus on behavior rather than personality and, if possible, avoid labeling people as outstanding, average, or poor performers. Most likely, your company will still make you rate your perception of each employee on several subjective, pre-determined attributes, such as interpersonal skills and job knowledge. Sadly, the company will then use these same attributes across a broad range of jobs that differ greatly in skills and knowledge required.

Most likely, you will be told to rate employees on a five-to-seven-point scale. Many companies want supervisors to rate most employees in the middle ("meets expectations" range) and to give very few excellent scores as a means to keep raises as low as possible. Some companies make it very difficult for managers to award employees an excellent score; this is reserved for "water walkers." Needless to say, having a rating point that nobody can reach is senseless, and will force you to spend time explaining to your best employees why you cannot give them a top rating.

Employees, in turn, want higher ratings on attributes and job performance to earn a larger raise. With a five-point scale, employees will perceive 1 as an F, 3 as a C, and 5 as an A. While the company thinks a rating of 3 (meets expectations) is quite satisfactory, nobody wants a C. The annual review can be very destructive if you rate someone below what they think is fair.

So, given that you may have to comply with these crazy attribute ratings, here are some tips on how to do it most productively:

Rating the attributes

Discuss each attribute listed on the rating sheet. Start out by letting the employee tell you how he thinks he should be rated and why. Then add your thoughts and come to a mutual agreement on the rating. Try your best not to demotivate the employee. Criticism tends to result in the person going on the defensive and reacting emotionally.

Ask yourself how important it is that the employee be made aware of your perception. Do not force the issue on a minor point unless the employee has performed especially poorly on an important attribute. And if that is the case, you should have already been coaching the employee to improve long before the annual performance review. If both of you agree that one of attributes deserves a low rating, discuss how improvement can be made.

For most employees simply use the annual review to motivate and build self-esteem. When rating attributes, get through them as quickly and simply as possible.

Primary goals and major accomplishments

Ask employees to briefly review their major goals and how successful they were in meeting them. Then discuss their list of major accomplishments for the past year. Listen closely and compliment them on major accomplishments. Tell employees they should be proud of their work and that you hope to give them more opportunities to achieve in the future. This is your chance to build their confidence and self-esteem.

Responsibility table

Guided by the employees' responsibility table, ask them how well they think they are doing in each area, what they like doing the most and the least, where they could use more help, and how you can better work together to get the desired results.

Listen carefully, paraphrase to clarify and then add your thoughts. Discuss any issues or responsibility changes that could be made to improve the job or work process. Discuss responsibilities in-depth at monthly or quarterly meetings where you have more time.

Employee development

Finally, at the end of the review, discuss the employee's personal growth within the department and the company and their professional aspirations. Jointly develop a training and education plan for the following year.

All of the above is not to say you should be entirely lenient during the annual review. Most people want to know where they stand in the eyes of their supervisor, so tell them. But again, if they are doing poorly in some aspect of the job, they should have already been made aware of it before the annual review.

Monthly Reviews

I strongly suggest that you conduct monthly or at least quarterly reviews with each employee, depending on how much coaching is needed and on how frequently you must be kept informed on major projects and goals. These meetings are important for you to monitor progress, provide feedback, set and review goals, delegate new projects and responsibilities, and for coaching.

Below are some topics that can be handled productively at monthly or quarterly meetings with individual employees:

- *Set goals:* Individual goals are usually set once a year right after corporate goals are issued. However, as circumstances change you may want to modify them occasionally.
- *Review goal progress:* Do this at least quarterly. Let the employee update you on the status of each major goal. If

goals are not being met, discuss and coach the worker on how to improve. Then meet a month later to make sure those changes have indeed been implemented.

- *Discuss major projects:* Let the employee update you on each major assignment or project: timelines, unforeseen problems, additional resources needed to get the job done, and any other issues that may come up. Plan together how to keep the projects on track (or get them back on track, as needed).
- *Delegate new assignments or projects:* When delegating new responsibilities, make sure you explain them in detail, including what you expect to be done, when and why. The more employees understand the big picture and the importance of the project, the higher their commitment will be.
- *Discuss and modify responsibilities:* Use the employee responsibility table as a guideline to discuss how things are going in each of the employee's major areas of responsibility. Let them give you a status update, including any problems encountered that require coaching. Listen carefully without interruption, and then coach. Discuss the responsibilities the employee likes best and least, and why. Modify responsibilities when necessary, especially when enriching jobs.

Chapter 10 Takeaway

- Since people can never separate their rational from their emotional selves, do your best to conduct the review in a way that minimizes emotional reactions.
- Despite the pitfalls of annual reviews, most companies require them. Make the employees feel safe enough to have an open and honest discussion.
- Minimize negative comments to keep people from becoming defensive and angry. Try to build self-esteem, give encouragement, and correct minor problems.
- Avoid surprises. Major problems should be addressed long before the annual review. Do tell people where they are doing a good job and where they need to improve.
- When discussing attributes, let the employee talk first, then come to a mutual agreement. Do not waste time and create ill feelings over minor points.
- Discuss how well goals and responsibilities were met, acknowledge achievements, and review employee development needs.

Managing Your Boss

YOUR relationship with your supervisor is vitally important to your success and survival within your company. As previously mentioned, 70 percent of the people who leave their jobs do it because of their immediate supervisor. People do not quit jobs—they quit bosses. Regardless of the type of supervisor you have, that person holds the upper hand, so it is up to you to build the relationship. Set your ego aside, think about what your supervisor expects from you, and work to build a good relationship.

If your boss is especially difficult, you may look for another job, quit, or perhaps seek a transfer; but none of these are easy solutions. The best thing to do for the time being is to work hard to develop the type of relationship where you have no reason to quit and the supervisor has no reason to fire you.

What Supervisors Want

As a manager, think about what you want from your employees. You want them to be at work on time, get their work done on time with high quality, meet their goals, voice few complaints, cause no trouble, keep you informed, manage their budgets, get along with coworkers, and never criticize you or make you look bad in public. Your boss wants the same things from you.

Furthermore, your boss wants to know that your department is functioning well, so he does not have to worry about it. If it is, you as manger get the credit; and if not, you get the blame. It's as simple as that.

If you take note of the management ideas presented in this guide and apply them, you should have an efficient, effective top-notch department that is not a concern for your boss.

Building a Relationship

Here are some of the things you should be doing to make your supervisor happy, like and respect you, and consider you a valuable employee.

Inform

Keep your supervisor informed so as to avoid surprises. Ask him what information he wants to see (metrics), how he wants to be kept informed (reports or meetings) and how often (weekly, monthly, quarterly). Then make sure to provide that information consistently.

Let your supervisor know how well your department is meeting goals on a monthly or quarterly basis, even if he did not ask for it. Knowing that your department is being run successfully is reassuring to your boss and good for your relationship.

Expand your job

Talk to you supervisor about any work you could take off his plate. Ask him to delegate whole jobs that will give you more responsibility while freeing up some of his time. The act of asking, by itself, should enhance his opinion of you.

When the supervisor does ask for help, volunteer for the job. Supervisors like people who step up to help. Moreover, you want to expand your job anyway. This will be good for your career.

Be flexible

Supervisors will do little things that drive you nuts. This may happen because they are busy and sometimes forget to handle things appropriately. They may request a last-minute report, ask that you attend a spur-of-the-moment meeting, give a presentation to outside guests, or expect you to undertake something that requires more time than they realize. Try to minimize your emotional reaction and accept the fact that these inconveniences will happen occasionally. Then work through them as part of your job.

While working in the Chicago area, my supervisor in Florida would occasionally summon me to meetings. Sometimes I arrived in Florida only to discover that the meeting was canceled. At first it was very annoying. But once I accepted the fact that anything could happen, I flew prepared and nothing surprised me.

Like it or not, it is the supervisors' ballpark that you are playing in, and if you do not like it, you may need to find another ballpark. My advice is to expect anything and be flexible. By asking for more work you are setting yourself up for last minute assignments. Accept them as part of your job.

Supervisors can sometimes interfere by bypassing you and going directly to your employees. It is up to you then to determine how much of an impact this has on your people. If it happens only occasionally, it may actually make them feel important, so ignore the interference. But if it is a frequent occurrence and has a negative impact on the work your employees are doing, then you need to address it openly and tactfully with your supervisor. Explain why that behavior is a problem and why it would be beneficial for work requests to go through you instead.

Contribute

Good supervisors will expect you to contribute to departmental and other meetings. Speak up and state your point of view in a factual, non-threatening manner, and try to keep your emotions in check.

Support

Give your supervisor sincere support whenever possible. Most supervisors want honest opinions and support, not just yes men or women. Tell the truth and speak up when appropriate, but be aware of your supervisor's style. Some bosses are more open to honest opinion than others.

Supervisors like employees who are loyal and supportive. Avoid arguments with your supervisor, especially in public. Never talk about him behind his back because doing so could easily get back to him. If you disagree with a decision of his, present your argument, but once the final decision is made, make sure to support it.

Show up

Supervisors want their employees to show up on time and do their jobs well with as little hassle as possible. Show up every day, do your job and do not bother your supervisor with minor issues.

Handling Conflicting Beliefs

Confronting your supervisor or senior executives about their beliefs can result in career suicide. Still, you should question bad decisions if you feel strongly enough and are confident you have the information to make your case. Approach your supervisor or top management with reverence, explaining that you respectfully disagree and why (bad assumptions, incorrect strategies, etc.). Make your case logically and discuss the advantages of your position for the company.

Sometimes this approach works and sometimes it does not. If you supervisor is the type who is always right, you will know it before you try to resolve an issue. Only you can decide if this issue is worth putting your job on the line. Sometimes you may choose not to pick a battle. Focus on the challenge of being the best manager you can be and keep good documentation in case you need it later.

Chapter 11 Takeaway

- A good relationship with your boss is critical to your success, and it is your responsibility to build it. Show up on time, produce timely, high-quality results, meet your goals, refrain from criticism, and manage your budget.
- Let your supervisor know your department is functioning well. Avoid surprises, provide status reports, volunteer for assignments, be flexible, participate in meetings, be loyal and supportive, never argue in public, and never make your boss look bad.
- Supervisors can be difficult, so minimize your emotional reactions and accept their behavior as part of the job.
- When you disagree with your supervisor or senior management, proceed respectfully and with caution. Gather data to support your position and present your case objectively. Once you have made your case, support the final decision.

Epilogue

W HAT would you say if your HR department, your employees, or your supervisor asked you to describe your management style and the way you plan to work with them? Now that you have read and studied this guide, here is what I hope you would tell them.

To the HR Department

Whenever I have a position to fill I will work closely with you and devote as much time as necessary to executing our plan to find, interview and hire the best possible candidates. I make this commitment because my first responsibility as a manager is to hire the right people into the right positions. This can only happen if I work closely with you. If I do not accomplish this goal, my department will always be mediocre, no matter what else I do.

To My Department

I practice a management style that assumes that each of you wants to work, learn, use your talents, accept responsibility, make decisions, solve problems, achieve, and grow in your job.

As your manager, my real job is to get the work of our department done through you, not to do it myself. I will delegate everything I can that is challenging and meaningful, which should help you grow in your jobs. By delegating I will also free more of my time to do the things only a manager can and should do..

At times problems will arise in the workplace. Most likely they will involve company policies or administrative issues, supervision, relationships, work conditions, salary, or benefits. I expect you to help me identify problems so that we can correct them. Please remember that none of these factors, not even salary and benefits, are motivators; but I do want them to be fair and equitable.

What will truly motivate you are meaningful, challenging jobs and the sense of achievement you feel from doing your work well. As your manager, enriching your jobs is one of my top priorities. Without a good job that gives you opportunities to achieve, you cannot be motivated. Therefore, I plan to give you plenty of responsibility, autonomy and opportunities to achieve. And when you do, you will be recognized for your accomplishments.

To give you exposure and help you progress within the company, I will ask you to present your own work results to others whenever appropriate. Therefore I encourage you to get comfortable with public speaking. At our internal meetings, I would like you to speak up, present your ideas, offer solutions to problems, and give your honest opinion. But once we reach a decision, I expect you to support it.

I plan to hold staff meeting at least monthly. To keep them productive and not waste your time, we will always have an agenda. I know you want to be kept "in the know," so I will keep you informed on company issues as much as possible.

At times we will have internal conflicts. But rather than hide them, I plan to discuss them openly, without a threat to anyone who speaks up. Working through our differences should lead to a better understanding of each point of view, and may even change some of our beliefs or attitudes and resolve the conflict. Open discussions may bring about consensus with genuine commitment, or even an innovative solution.

I realize that most of you hate annual performance reviews. But since they are required, I will try to structure them so they are productive and not intimidating. We will mainly discuss your responsibilities, achievements, and your career development goals.

To Each Employee

I hope we can develop mutual trust so we can have two-way communication, listen to each other, and openly discuss our points of view. We will work together to finalize your job description and responsibility table so that we both clearly understand your duties and responsibilities. Together we will set your annual goals so they are clear, challenging, reachable, and consistent with our departmental goals.

On a monthly or quarterly basis we will review your goal progress to be sure you're on track. I'm here to coach you, so if you have any problems, please ask for help. Then we can discuss the issues and consider the alternative solutions.

The major reasons for poor motivation at work are having a bad job, a bad boss, or inappropriate training. So I want to be sure none of these happen. I will try to give you a job with responsibility for an entire piece of work, not just a portion, and as much autonomy as possible regarding when and how your work gets done. If further training or education is needed to help you succeed, I will provide it.

When you think about your job and your goals, please try to identify the vital few truly important activities you do that lead to success in reaching your goals and focus on addressing those. Also, try to identify what we call the "trivial many" activities you do that contribute little or nothing to your success and are just a waste of time. Drop them.

To My Boss

It is very important that we have a good working relationship. I want you to feel confident that my department is running smoothly, maintains high quality, gets the work done on time, and meets our goals. I want to build your trust so you won't worry about me or about my department.

I plan to show up for work on time, meet our goals as scheduled while delivering high quality, stay within budget, keep you informed so you have no surprises, not bother you with minor issues, and support you in any way possible.

I will keep you informed on department issues and progress as frequently as you like. Please let me know what information (budget, productivity, goal progress, etc.) and metrics you would like to see, and how often you would like to receive a report or meet with me in person.

Whenever you have any work assignments or projects that I can take off your plate, please let me know.

About the Author

Steven R. Smith, R.PH, M.S., was raised in Nelson, a small Wisconsin town near the Mississippi River. He attended high school in Alma, Wisconsin, graduated in 1961 in a class of only 37, and went on to earn a B.S. in pharmacy and an M.S. in pharmacy administration, both from the University of Wisconsin-Madison.

Smith started his career in 1968 as a marketing research analyst at the Upjohn Company in Kalamazoo, Michigan, and then held positions as market analyst, product manager and new products manager at Ross Laboratories and Abbott Laboratories.

Smith held his first managerial position in 1978, when he was hired to establish a marketing research department at American Critical Care, a small cardiovascular drug company in the Chicago area. Subsequently, Smith held licensing positions at American Critical Care, G.D. Searle, and Fujisawa Healthcare. He also taught marketing and management classes.

More recently Smith served as vice president of business development at Miles Laboratories in Elkart, Indiana, and Dow

Pharmaceutical Sciences in Petaluma, California. He is now retired and lives in Petaluma with Judy, his wife of 45 years.

15⁹⁹

CPSIA information can be obtained
at www.ICGtesting.com
Printed in the USA
LVOW13s1601100517
534024LV00010B/960/P